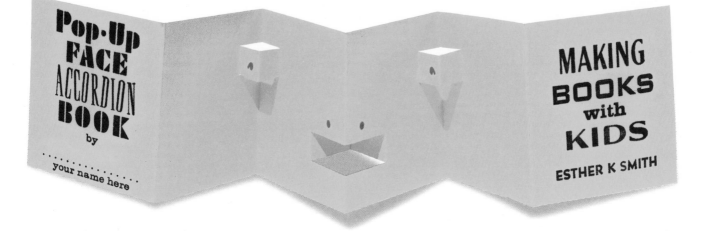

**Pop-Up
FACE
ACCORDION
BOOK**

by

. . . .
your name here

**MAKING
BOOKS
with
KIDS**

ESTHER K SMITH

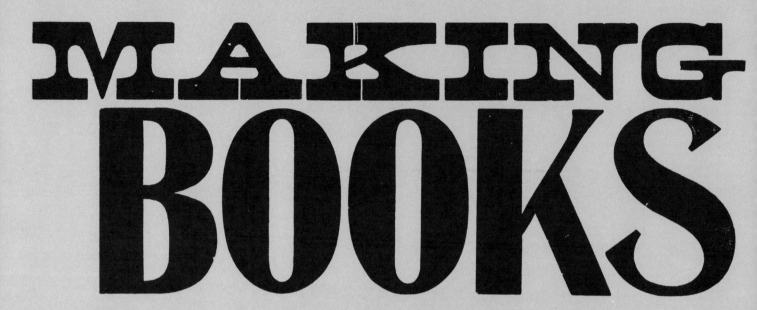

MAKING BOOKS

**25 Paper Projects
to fold, sew, paste,
pop, and draw**

QUARRY

with KIDS

by

ESTHER K SMITH

illustrations by Jane Sanders
type-o-graphics by Dikko Faust

Quarto is the authority on a wide range of topics.

Quarto educates, entertains and enriches the lives of
our readers—enthusiasts and lovers of hands-on living.

www.QuartoKnows.com

© 2016 Quarto Publishing Group USA Inc.
Text, projects, and photography © 2016 Esther K Smith
Illustrations © 2016 Jane Sanders, www.reddozer.com
Type-o-graphics © 2016 Dikko Faust, Purgatory Pie Press

First published in the United States of America in 2016 by
Quarry Books, an imprint of
Quarto Publishing Group USA Inc.
100 Cummings Center
Suite 406-L
Beverly, Massachusetts 01915-6101
Telephone: (978) 282-9590
Fax: (978) 283-2742
QuartoKnows.com
Visit our blogs at QuartoKnows.com.

ISBN: 978-1-63159-081-8

Digital edition published in 2016
eISBN: 978-1-62788-842-4

Library of Congress Cataloging-in-Publication Data available

Cover and book design: Esther K Smith, Dikko Faust, Amy Sly
Design production: Robin Sherin, Jane Treuhaft
Cover and book photography: Emma Andreetti, Wyatt Counts
Additional photography: Michael Bartalos, Han Ju Chou, Michael Prisco

Printed in China

To the child in all of us—and to all the kids, and to all the grownups when you were kids, and to all the teachers and kids I have taught—including Larry when I was 10 and he was 4. And, of course, to little Georgia and little Polly—and Dikko as usual. And to Paul Faust age 96—the best father-in-law in the world ever—who chuckled when I told him I needed to write something inspiring (which he read on his TTY device for the hard of hearing) and said, "Good luck with THAT."

CONTENTS!

INTRODUCTION 8

1

BASICS 10

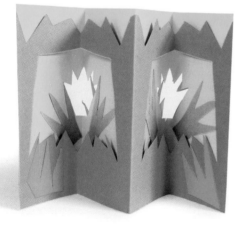

2

FOLDING BOOKS 24

3

MAKING POP-UPS 58

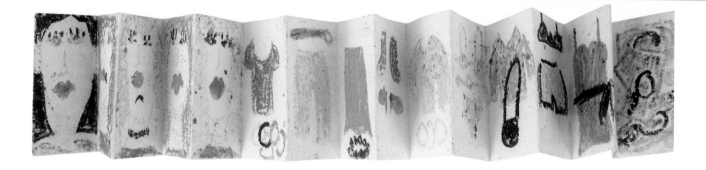

DECORATING PAPERS 88

SEWING BOOKS 104

INTRODUCTION

I was filling out forms in a waiting room. A little boy ran around, noisy and wild—he kept bumping me. When I finished the forms, I made him a book from a piece of paper. (I offered to show him how, but he said he was too young—he was a very tall 4½-year old.) The room got so quiet, I thought he had left. I looked around and he was still there—drawing and drawing. All of that bouncing, bounding energy absorbed in his project. I wish I could show you his beautiful book. I think this book he made with me will stay with him as he grows. He may not remember it, but he spent more than 30 minutes writing his book. I left before he had finished.

When I was a child, my mother and I would cut paper angels when I was home sick from school. My dad and I twisted moebius strips from silver paper package liners. When we cut them one way, they doubled in size. Cut the other direction, they became two interlocking loops. In school we'd make paper Kleenex flowers for Mother's Day. And we'd trace shapes onto colored papers to cut out and decorate with glitter, and tape to the windows to celebrate the seasons.

I hand make books and limited editions at Purgatory Pie Press with my husband, Dikko Faust. When our younger child was a baby, we moved to our current studio. (I think we got the studio because she was so cute—the elevator man liked her.) We corralled a sunny area with toys and a little chair. But the baby just stood at the fence miserable and crying. So we corralled the printing press and the small metal type and dangerous stuff instead. It was perfect. Dikko could step over it. I worked on the counters and the baby had the floor—like a timeshare only vertical. Whatever she could reach was hers. What she couldn't get into was mine.

Our older child came to the studio after kindergarten and would bring friends. Our paper trimmings were their toys. One day the kids cut scraps of thin rag paper into money and drew their own dollars. I was tempted to print an edition of that. Hmmm—maybe I can find some kid to draw money now.

Our apartment was too small—we went to the parks to play. But the kids and I would sit at our kitchen table and cut paper and draw. One afternoon, when I opened the mail, I took my scissors and cut up all the envelopes and junk mail into creatures and spiral snakes and flowers and vines. My daughter loved it. She took them to school for Show and Tell.

When we moved to a larger apartment, we found a big yellow vintage table in an antique store on our way to a friend's art exhibit. That became our work and play table. We would clear it for meals—or at least push our projects off to the side. We made sock dolls together as well as paper things. One holiday, I opened a gift box to find a doll—with several changes of clothes. My younger daughter had secretly sewn it in her bed at night. From hanging around making things with us, our children had learned so much: how to make things, how to organize their own projects, how to figure things out.

Children do not know they can't do things. This can be tough when they are two-years old. But when you realize it's their beginning of independence, you can make sure they are safe and give them control of enough to satisfy them. When they are a little older, making things with them is a great way to encourage self-reliance.

At a concert last summer, I met a woman wearing origami paper earrings that she had folded. She works as a child therapist. Her clients are homeless children and kids in foster care. She said she sometimes teaches them origami forms—just so they can have something. She told me one girl said she wished she owned a book. I taught her a simple book form so she could show them, and they could always have a book.

Back in that same waiting room a few days ago, I showed a father and his eight-year-old son how to make a book. The boy's first one was a mess, but right away he made another one that was 100 times better—and then he and his dad each made one more. The father said, "It was worth it to come here just for this."

Have fun with your kids. *Esther*

MAKE BOOKS NOT WAR

1 BASICS

his chapter is like my first class when I teach—lots of background and things you need to know before you begin the fun part. Here I am giving you the information you need to make the projects that follow. First the parts of the book, then paper and tools.

I am the kind of person who is raring to go so skips things over and maybe feels bad later. Today I ran out of switchel when my friend Jen was visiting. I pulled out the cider vinegar, ginger, and honey and said—"I could look it up or just go for it." Jen said "LOOK IT UP"—she said, "When you've made it a few times, you will remember it." And so true—better not to waste in haste.

At New York City's Center for Book Arts back when they were on Bleecker Street, in the very beginning, the founder Richard Minsky made bookbinder Mindell Dubansky a sign that said MINDY REMEMBER SLOW IS FAST. So don't skip this. Read it over and come back to it as you need to when you are making the books with your kids.

PARTS OF A BOOK

Just to keep things clear—here is some basic vocabulary to identify parts of a book.

You probably already know SPINE—it's where the pages attach to each other. On commercial books and many handmade books, the title is on the spine so you can find them on your bookshelf.

Opposite the spine is the FORE EDGE—the front edge of the pages of book.

The top edge of the book pages is called the HEAD.

The bottom edge of the book pages is called the TAIL.

SIGNATURES are the folded sections that make up the inside of the book. Pamphlet books have one signature, but books like the one you are now reading are multi-signature—and the sections are stitched together. This book (unless things change) has nine 16-page signatures.

ENDSHEETS, also called ENDPAPERS, are the papers between the cover and the inside of the book. These papers can be pretty and colorful.

FLYLEAF is the name for the inside endsheet that turns next to the book's pages.

Paper

You can use many kinds of paper. What is lying around? In the United States, letter paper, lightweight business/printer paper is handy. In other countries A4 is standard letter paper. For trying things out, like simple pop-ups, you could use the back of paper that's printed on one side.

You can reuse paper bags. Opaque color markers, stamp pad inks, and gouache look beautiful on brown paper. They almost glow—maybe because the color value is close to the medium tone of the kraft paper. What we have in the United States is different from other countries—but everywhere there is some unbleached paper that people use for wrapping, and that can be very nice for kid's art. Brown paper and butcher and bakery papers come in rolls. Rolls can be hard to control, too sproingy, but you could find a dispenser—or rig something with a little rope.

Warning: Some papers are brittle. Newsprint just does not work well for books—and I am sad to say that construction paper, with those pretty colors, is often very high in acid and, like newsprint, is too brittle to fold well. Now there are some good alternative color papers. One colleague who works with kids recommends Tru-Ray.

Everyone's talking about archival. Archival's a difficult word. Archive just means to keep things in some organized way. For Purgatory Pie Press's archive, in addition to the interesting art and poetry and letters, preliminary drawings, etc., we have kept the phone and electric bills, not printed on fancy papers.

ACIDITY is the issue. High-acid papers are not good for making art. They are brittle. They crack when you try to fold them. *Acid-free* is the term for what some people call archival.

Scrapbook makers have made acid-free papers, pens, glues, and tapes available for everyone. Maybe that's because artists can be intimidated by fancy materials— so the best things happen on the backs of envelopes. But scrapbooks are meant to be archives for the future, so the purpose is different.

Typical letter/printer/copier paper is pretty good. But anything that's been around for a while is either brittle (don't use it) or OK. Don't spend a fortune on paper— but use papers that will not crumble before your kids are old enough to appreciate what they made when they were younger.

It's fun to buy decorative papers, but simple whites and colors that are the same on both sides. You want papers that are a good weight for folding. For books like pocket accordions, very lightweight is good. For other things, use sturdier papers that are thin enough to fold or cut with scissors—light cover weight, card stocks, etc.

Get to know your local printer. Printers buy full cartons of paper, but may not use it all. Printers also trim jobs after printing. Those trimmings may be plenty big enough for making books.

When I chose Japanese paper for our wedding invitation, New York Central art supply store asked me to work in the paper department. I took the job to learn more about paper. If you have a good art supply store, someone there may be a paper expert. Get to know them. If corners are damaged, they may sell that paper cheap— or even donate it to your cause.

Paper Grain

Understanding paper grain is important. In paper manufacturing, a thin, porridgy slurry flows down artificial streams. The fibers line up with the flow of the water— and the paper well folds along those fibers or with the grain. Paper does not fold well against the grain—folding against the grain is frustrating—for small hands this is even worse.

Take a piece of paper and without looking at it, roll one edge, and then roll the perpendicular edge. Can you feel which side rolls with less resistance? It may be easier to feel if you roll a stack of paper.

Or cut out a small piece, near a corner, drawing a line through it before you cut so that you can put it back where it was. Dampen that piece to see how it curls as it dries. It will curl with the grain. Put the piece back where it was, matching the line you drew, to kow the grain for your whole piece of paper.

Tearing is another way to test paper grain. When I want to tear a story out of a newspaper, it tears really well one direction and I feel so skillful—and then it goes crazy when I tear the other way. It tears better with the grain, than against it.

Signatures

The basic unit of many book structures (including the one you are holding) is the signature—a folded section of paper. Commercial books are trimmed on the fore edge. But fancier commercial books are not trimmed—there is a little ripple on the fore edge from all those signature arrows. Patti Smith's *Just Kids* paperback had an untrimmed fore edge to give it panache. For one of my how-to books, I asked for that, but they told me it cost extra in production and would have raised the price of the book. I did not want my readers to have to pay extra just for a little panache. But it's funny that NOT

How To Fold Signatures

Fold a piece of paper in half, you get 4 pages—Magic! 2=8, 3=12, 4=16. Crazy math! How many pages you put in a signature depends on the thickness of your paper. For typical printer paper, 4-6 sheets should work. Experiment and see what you like.

materials

paper, a few sheets
bone folder

1 To make a signature, stack a few sheets of paper, keeping the sheets flush at the bottom.

2 Fold the stack in half along the grain (for more on grain, see page 13).

3 Before you crease, check the fore edge—you will see that the inside sheet sticks out just a little, and the outside sheet is just a touch shorter. It should be symmetrical, like an arrow if you look at it from above.

When children are learning to fold, this symmetry is not a high priority—but as they get older, with more eye-hand coordination and experience, they can do this.

Some people want to be very neat and think folding each sheet by itself is worth the extra time. The trouble is that when you put your sheets together to form the signature, the outer one still needs to go around all the rest—so if you have a sharp fold, it will not help.

trimming costs more than trimming in commercial book production. If you trim the fore edge of a handmade book, it is hard work—and if your knife slips, it can wreck your book. I don't think it's worth it—especially for books that kids make.

The amount of paper in a signature depends on the weight or thickness of the paper. The book you are holding (unless it's the e-book version) has 16-page signatures—that is four sheets of lightweight paper, folded in half. A math textbook might have 32-page signatures—on thinner paper. Something huge like a *Complete Shakespeare* or a *Compact Oxford English Dictionary*, printed on very, very thin paper could have even more pages per signature.

When you work with thick paper that still folds well—like 90-lb (244 gsm) cover weight—one folded sheet could be enough for a signature.

Attention to the paper grain is crucial for folding signatures. If you ever need to fold against the grain, score first. But really—just design your project according to your paper's grain. I cannot say enough how important it is to have kids work with grain-appropriate paper. If

I as a child—the motivated daughter of an artist, born with a crayon in my hand—found folding against the grain frustrating, it is something that can really discourage a kid who is already more interested in glowing screens.

I have been a guest artist in classrooms where I designed a project based on the grain of the paper, only to have the paper provided the wrong grain. The results were distressing. The kids struggle and then give up—or don't like what they make because it's so crooked.

Endsheets or Endpapers and Flyleaf

When you make the decorative papers in chapter 4, you can use those for endsheets. Since both sides will show, you could decorate both sides (let the first side dry before turning it over)—or lightly paint the back. If a book is simple and plain inside, very decorative endsheets can be the interesting colorful element. For a complex colorful book, you could use simple plain endpapers—a solid color—or just some interesting texture—to contrast and give your eyes a change from the book.

I first chose an endsheet when I designed my first limited-edition book with Dikko Faust, the founder of Purgatory Pie Press, where we make limited editions and artist books. It was a colorful Japanese paste stencil print—Katazome-shi. We matched our ink colors to that paper. What will I design for the endsheets of this book? Maybe Jane the illustrator will draw something. Or we could make a pattern. Or find some pretty decorative paper that we can use. Take a look at the endsheets now to see what I chose. (If you have the e-book version, I will tell the publisher I promised to include the endsheets.)

Basic Tools

You need a few basic tools to make books. You may even be able to do without some, but tools are a small investment that can make your life easier. Keep them in a nice box if you can. It will put you in the right mood to make books. MY tool box is from South Africa, made from tin cans—JAPANESE tin cans.

Glue and Paste

There are so many glues. Some glues are very bad for paper—raising its acidity. Some glues are flammable and toxic—even when they do not smell bad—so read the labels on your glue. One student brought in clear, odorless glue. I was suspicious because it was not familiar and it seemed too good to be true. I read the label and the warnings were dire—but so nicely designed we might never have noticed the warnings.

Do Not Use Rubber Cement. It is not safe to breathe. And it rots your paper. I did not heed Richard Olson, my printmaking professor, who warned against rubber cement—and then I saw everything I had glued and mounted with rubber cement turn brown in a couple of years.

Glue sticks—acid-free, photo safe, permanent (but NOT removable)—are great for trying out projects. Burnish them well and they can work. Burnishing means rubbing your paper with a bone folder after you fold or glue. I put real strength into burnishing for sharp folds and to encourage my glue and paste to absorb into the paper fibers.

Acid-free, double-stick tapes can also work well—*photo safe* is one of the key words to look for when choosing tapes and glues that will not damage your art.

Making your own wheat paste is fast and cheap and easy—but children tend to goop it on. A thin coat is

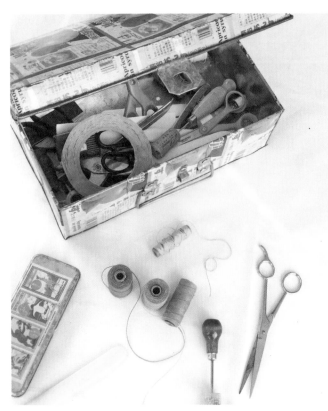

plenty—not an easy concept for kids. Wheat paste is not sticky and takes patience. The other hard part about inexperienced people using wheat paste is drying. Paste is slow to dry. Paste dampens your paper, and the paper can buckle. You need to set it under weights (see page 22) with waste sheets. Waste sheets are pieces of clean, cheap paper—can be newsprint—magazine pages, backs of printer paper. And you must keep changing the waste sheets again and again until it dries.

You can make your own wheat paste (see opposite page). You can also buy instant paste mix. And I was tempted when our first child was a baby to try using baby rice cereal as paste. It might work. For the second child, we gave her a banana as her first solid. That also could probably stick papers together, but I do not recommend it.

Wheat Paste

This paste can be used for paste papers as well as bookbinding, and it is perfect for bookplates—just brush it on very thin.

materials

unbleached flour or corn starch
water
1 clove (the scent discourages insects—
   remove it after you cook your paste)
measuring cups and spoons
stirring spoon and/or whisk
cooking pot or double boiler +/or
   microwave-safe bowl
stove or microwave
storage containers
refrigerator

1 Mix one part flour with six parts water until smooth. You can use cornstarch instead of flour, with a 1:12 ratio of starch to water.

Throw in that clove if you like.

2 Cook and stir until it thickens and turns translucent. It can scorch, so you may want to use a double boiler—or just don't stop stirring. This is like making pudding.

3 Cover and refrigerate whatever you do not use within a few hours. Paste does not last long.

NOTE: For small quantities, you can cook it in a plastic take-out container in a microwave, pausing to stir every 15 seconds or so. When I need just a bit, I use 1 teaspoon of flour to 2 tablespoons of water. For paste papers, we make larger amounts—and those are slow to cook in a microwave.

This paste is good for paper collages. Brush on very thin coats—less is more! It is not sticky, but holds when dry.

For large pasted areas, you need to layer with waste sheets to absorb dampness and then weight it. Keep changing the waste sheets to absorb the dampness. If it feels cool to the touch, it is not quite dry.

How to Glue Collage Pieces

Whether you are using a glue stick or a brush with paste or glue, there are some tricks that make gluing a collage easier. I sometimes keep a damp rag on my work table to clean my fingers as I work.

materials

collage pieces
waste sheets (an old phone book if those still exist—or a magazine or the backs of printouts)
photo-safe glue stick or brush and paste (see wheat paste recipe on page 17)
paper or book to collage onto
bone folder

1 Lay your collage pieces upside down on a piece of waste paper.

2 Coat the collage back with a very thin coat of paste. Paste out to the edge of all your collage pieces, letting the gluestick or paste brush go onto the waste paper.

3 With great care, lift each collage piece and place it onto your book. Cover the collage with a clean piece of waste paper and burnish it with your bone folder.

4 Replace the waste paper with another clean piece. Be sure no glue or paste seeps out from the edges of your collage pieces.

Put your book under a weight (see page 22). Keep a piece of wax paper next to the collage while it is under a weight in case any glue seeps out.

5 When your collage no longer feels cool to the touch, it is dry.

NOTE: Another method is to scan and print or color photocopy your pieces on a single sheet of paper, back it with dry adhesive, then cut your shapes out and use them like stickers.

Bone Folders

Bone folders are not expensive—they start around five dollars. You can buy them from many art stores or online. Some are bone, some horn. Some are Teflon—they cost a lot but have special uses for professional binders, since they do not shine the paper when you fold it. You can use a piece of waste paper when you burnish to avoid that shine—but for kids' work, you do not really need to worry about that.

Other bone folders are plastic or melamine. Sometimes melamine costs more than the real bone. Beware of beautiful packages with melamine contents. But it's not animal. Unless you think of fossil fuel as prehistoric bones. But Peter D. Verheyen, who runs the Book Arts List Serve, says fossil fuels are generally plant based.

Kids can use craft sticks, tongue depressors, or spoons for burnishing. But bone folders are also good for scoring and embossing and ripping paper—which I like to do instead of cutting. When I was a child, I rubbed down folds with my fingers. I remember my mother using her fingernails—mine were too soft.

Threads

Use real linen bookbinding thread. It comes on spools with so much that it is cheaper than other threads by the yard. An all-cotton button thread might be also OK.

I like waxing thread—partly because I like the smell of beeswax. To wax your thread, pull a length of thread through a lump of beeswax. I get beeswax from the farmers' market. (I also use it for greasing cookie sheets, but that's another book.) I mail order some of my waxed linen thread—that does not smell like beeswax.

You can buy plain unwaxed linen thread and dye it different colors with household dye—use take-out containers in the microwave. Just loosely tie little bundles, dampen them, dip them in hot dye, or cook for a minute in the microwave, and then pull them out, rinse in cold water (follow directions on the dye packages), and hang to dry. At a silkscreen studio where I taught, they dyed thread, dipping it into cups of silkscreen ink—but that may not be available where you are. Whatever you have, you can try it. But I did not do well dying my thread in fountain pen ink or with cranberries—and the Rit dye worked.

Test your thread to see if it is good and strong before you use it to make a book. You could test your other thread this way before you sew clothing too—to avoid humiliation.

Here's how to test thread: Wrap it a few times around the fingers on both hands, pull it, and try to snap it. If you can, it's not strong enough. If you feel like you will cut your fingers before the thread breaks, it's good thread.

Needles

Buy dull needles—tapestry or darning needles—with eyes that are big enough for your thread.

Sometimes, I have found myself threading needles for everyone in my class. If you already sew, you are comfortable with things like threading needles—but there are a few differences with sewing books. We use single thread, and we do not tie a knot, but knot our threads together later—that way the thread pulls against thread instead of the knot pushing through the paper fibers.

There is a way to lock your thread onto your needle so that it does not come unthreaded (see page 109). Once I learned to do that, I also found it useful for sewing hems.

Awls

Many people do not know the name of this basic tool. An awl is a sharp needle set into a handle—like a screwdriver.

Because sharp needles can so easily poke the wrong hole, bookbinders use awls to make sewing holes—then stitch with blunt needles. That way you do not pierce your paper by mistake—or prick your fingers as you sew.

Awls are sharp and my editor Joy wants me to warn you not to poke out your eye. Don't let kids run around with awls—use them in a calm, controlled setting.

You want an awl with a thin, straight point. You can also use potters needles or etching needles. And if you are working with a bunch of kids, pushpins or T-pins can work.

Since bookbinding has become popular, tools are sold in many art stores. And some of my students have bought a very pretty awl with an egg-shaped wooden handle. The points tend to snap on these—maybe because the handle allows too much pressure? Plus they cost more. So tell your store that Esther K Smith says those are not good ones and they should get the stronger, cheaper awls.

I have a bunch of awls in my toolbox for students who forget to bring theirs and I was hurting my fingers reaching in—until at a book fair at Pyramid Atlantic near Washington, D.C., I met a bookbinder who told me she uses wine corks to protect the tips of her awls. I said I did not drink much wine—and the next day at my book fair table, I found a big bag of corks—she and her husband have a bottle of wine with dinner every night.

Scissors

I saw a family on the New York City subway—tourists with a big, heavy stroller, a mother with her baby, and her mother, and her grandmother—four generations—speaking a language with shw's. I was shy to ask, but I think they were Polish. They had beautiful, broad cheekbones—and were lovely and plump.

The mother carried the baby—and when someone gave them a seat, she pulled out her smartphone (protected with an impressive bumper) and handed it to the baby. This child, who was not old enough to walk onto the subway, held the screen and swiped with her fingers—she was an expert engaging with the phone.

This makes me think: When she is an adult, will she look back at smartphones the way we look back at typewriters? So quaint, so cool, so retro. What will the new device be then? And I think: Can she turn the pages of a book? Can she draw with a pencil? Can she cut with scissors?

I have taught many kids to cut with scissors. Every school pack of ten would have one pair for left-handed kids—and if your child is left-handed, you need to get those. I start by helping them hold the scissors. I draw lines of fringe around the edges of paper and help them cut fringe—one cut per line. Then we progress to simple shapes where they need to keep cutting—all this takes time, a few days of practice, a little at a time—and then they can cut. The Museum of Modern Art had an exhibit of Matisse's paper cuts. He used huge scissors—he grew up in an industrial textile family, working with tailors' sheers.

When I was a child, besides my blunt-tipped kids' scissors, we had my mother's scissors—loose and dull—and my father's scissors—sharp and not to be used on paper.

My fourth-grade Girl Scout troop made holiday wreathes. We had to cut plastic dry-cleaning bags into hundreds of 2" x 6" (5 x 15 cm) strips to tie over stretched wire hangers. My mother's scissors just could NOT cut that material without it catching—so the project was difficult and frustrating. But that was when I learned the value of good scissors. So I guess it was worth it.

Use good scissors for these projects. Help your kids learn to use them well and supervise their safety. Then when they are very old, like Matisse, if they get the urge they can hang out in a chair with gorgeous assistants making great art just by cutting.

Dull blades are more dangerous than sharp ones. That is not something I understood—until a dull knife slipped on some hard cheese and cut my thumb. UGH. So again—use the good scissors. Or get a good pair just for your paper projects. You may have a local place that sharpens knives and scissors. Fiskars makes affordable kids scissors—not super-cheap, but worth the price.

There are lots of scissors with crazy pattern blades—when I was a child, pinking shears were the only choice. Now the variety is overwhelming. But I found (after I invested in a bunch) that I don't use them. My simple, sharp scissors work best—one-use supplies do not seem worth the space they require. I say this from the perspective of a big-city apartment dweller—you may have plenty of room for one-use craft supplies.

One useful specialty scissor is tiny delicate nail scissors. For older kids, these can be great for detail work that would otherwise need to be done with a scalpel. I do not recommend knives for kids. And adults, even people very experienced working with knives, need to be so careful. I tell my students to also bring fingertip bandages when knives are involved. Me, I like tearing paper and cutting with scissors.

Some scissors now come with hard plastic blade covers. So I can carry scissors without having the blades poke through my handbag. This was nice when my subway got stuck after I'd seen the Matisse paper-cut exhibition. I cut my notebook paper into a Matisse-y snake until the train moved again.

When I travel, I always check my scissors and bookbinding tools with my luggage. Years ago my husband's 95-year-old grandmother had her crochet hook confiscated. It was big—she crocheted rag rugs. MAKE craft blog suggests always bringing a self-paid mailer so that anything that's not allowed on the plane can be sent to you and you don't lose your tools forever.

Corner Rounders

Bruno, who made some of the project samples for this book, loves to use corner rounders. And I agree, they are fun. I first started using them when I was helping in the bindery at the Metropolitan Museum. We rounded the corners of pamphlets and other things, not to be fancy, but because corners tend to get crushed—and the rounder ones are less vulnerable. There are some very nice heavy-duty corner rounders—a friend in California has an antique foot treadle model—but there are also some good cheap ones.

Book Weights

After you fold or glue, you need to "weight" your project. This means to put it under something heavy. There are many kinds of weights and many ways to make weights. You may already have paper weights or a heavy old clothes iron or heavy bookends. We have some beautiful geode bookends—our most useful wedding present—a gift from my sister-in-law, Sherry—thanks again, Sher.

Bookbinding studios have book presses, which, like Gutenberg's printing press, are related to cheese presses, wine presses, and flower presses, with a wheel that you tighten to increase the pressure.

Flat Weights

Use these to weight plain, folded or flat-glued surfaces like folded signatures or accordion books or glued hinges. Flat irons and paper weights can also work as book weights.

materials

heavy paper, or book cloth,
    or cloth, or orphan socks
glue and/or tape
something heavy—brick or
    cinderblock

Easiest method: stretch a sock around a brick. OR:

1 Wrap your brick or cinderblock with heavy paper or book cloth, like you are wrapping a present.

2 Glue or tape the wrapping paper or book-cloth shut.

Book Snakes

Weighting is tricky when you are gluing something three-dimensional onto your book. You can't just press it, or put it under a flat weight—that would crush it! This is when you need a soft, flexible weight—it can be something as simple as a bag of raw rice or split peas.

materials

fabric (can be a tightly woven sock or stocking)
dry rice, lentils, or buckwheat, clean sand, or fishing weights—buckshot can also work!
thread and needle or sewing machine
sharp, strong scissors

optional

plastic bag a little smaller than your sock or fabric

1 The easiest method is to find a tight-weave orphan sock with no holes. Then fill it loosely with rice or buckwheat or dried lentils or split peas or fishing weights.

2 Tie the open end shut. A more involved method is to turn in the open end, pin it, and sew it with a small whipstitch. Or you could topstitch on a sewing machine.

3 To prevent leaks you can put the weight into a plastic bag before inserting it into the sock.

This could also work with a tube of legging or tights material, or a sleeve from a long-sleeve T-shirt. Just be sure to tie or topstitch both ends.

4 Another slightly more complex method is to take a rectangle of fabric, fold it in half, right sides together, sew it like a bag on the bottom and the open side, letting the fold be your other side. Turn it right side out. Fill it with dry rice, peas, or weights. (Or a plastic bag full of rice, peas, etc.) Turn in the raw ends of the open side, and topstitch or whip stitch it closed. Because you do not want your rice, etc., to leak out, make small stitches that are close together and use tight-weave fabric.

Your weight can be whatever shape makes sense for you. Some people make snakes, which are also useful for holding open a book—like THIS book—as you read the directions and want your hands free to make the project. For a snake, make sure you use a long, narrow piece of fabric in step 4, fill it, and stitch it shut.

2 FOLDING BOOKS

Take a sheet of ordinary paper. Fold it in half. VOILA! You have 4 pages—front back, front back. Like magic. Folding is the basis of most books. And, for small children, folding can be one of the challenges. But the little fingers—feeling the texture of the paper, seeing the colors, preparing to draw their pictures, and writing their stories—will soon master this skill. Folding with the grain—not against the grain of the paper—is the most important thing you can do.

For some projects, like the Secret Pocket Accordion Book (page 26), you'll need to fold both with and against the grain. For those, use lightweight paper and pre-score if you need to.

Your bone folder is your basic tool—but fingers can be folders too. I remember rubbing things down with my fingers as my mother used her strong hard fingernails. A bone folder may slow you down at first—but when you get comfortable with it, it's like having an extra, very strong finger. I wish there was some tool that was like having an extra hand.

Perfectionism is the bane of creativity. It will take kids lots of practice to fold well. But they can still enjoy the books they make and treasure them later—even if the edges of the paper don't quite match. The important thing is for children to have the experience of learning to fold and making their own books. The important thing is what they put in their books, and how they get better at the craft with practice. And also how they will always know how to do this once they master it. The drawings they put in their books can be the beginning of stories they write later. The books they make now can be the beginning of architecture—building they will design or bridges they will engineer.

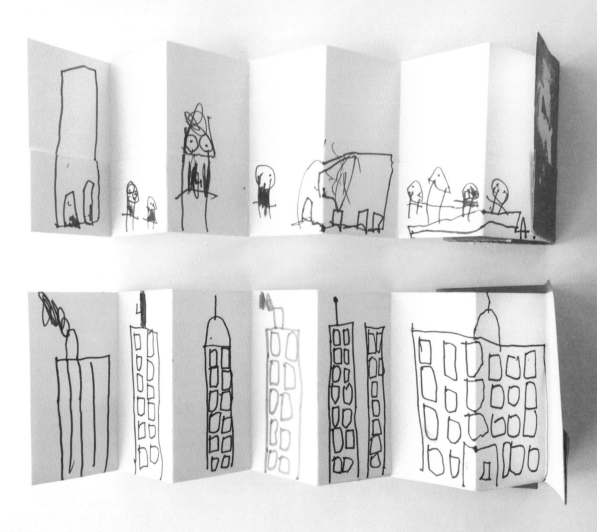

Secret Pocket Accordion Book

When I made these with kids at McNally Jackson Books in New York City, two brothers drew skyscrapers on their accordions, so that when they expanded—a city was standing there. What will you draw on yours? And what will you hide in your secret pockets?

materials

a long strip of lightweight paper, grain short
contrasting cover-weight paper, grain short and big enough to wrap around your folded pocket accordion
bone folder
straightedge
markers and/or collage supplies
glue and/or double-stick tape
scissors

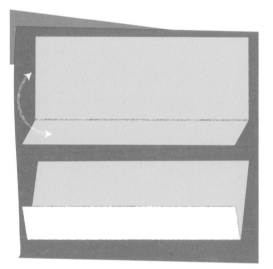

1 Pre-score your pocket on your paper about one-third up lengthwise as shown, using your straightedge and bone folder.

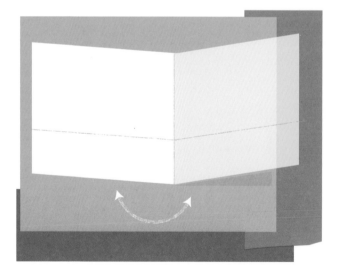

2 Fold up your pocket and burnish with the bone folder.

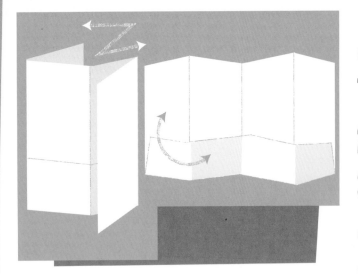

Cover

1 Pre-score a small pocket.

2 Fold up the pocket.

3 Unfold the pocket and fold in one side for a cover flap.

4 Open the flap and refold the pocket. Burnish with the bone folder.

5 Insert filled pocket accordion into cover flap pocket.

3 Open the pocket. Accordion-fold the paper to whatever size you like—if it does not come out even, the extra is good for attaching your cover.

4 Unfold your accordion. Refold the pocket. Refold your accordion with the pocket and burnish with your bone folder.

5 Decide: Do you want a secret pocket? If so, draw something innocent on the plain side. Draw something secret on the pocket side.

If the pocket is not a secret, you can draw on the pocket side.

Or collage your accordion, or both.

6 Gently fold your cover around your filled accordion; base your spine width on the thickest part of book. Allow enough space for the thickest part at the spine.

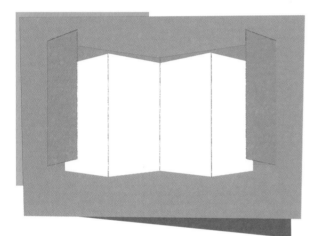

7 Fold in the other end of the accordion, and trim your cover as necessary to fit.

Or if the accordion did not come out evenly, glue that end into cover—either at the spine, or at the front or back.

When the inside accordion has its pockets and secret inserts, the cover folds around it and inserts itself into the cover pocket to stay shut.

Secret Treasure (Pockets for Pieces)

What would you like to keep in your pockets? Anything small and flat could work. Band-Aids, tiny origami, stickers, fortune-cookie fortunes, pictures cut from magazines, even balloons (before you blow them up)!

1 Find small secret treasures, or cut shapes smaller than your pockets and draw on them.

2 Fill your pocket accordion with secret treasures.

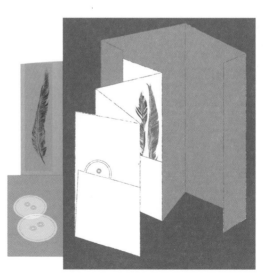

Skyscraper Accordion

Draw with scissors to make your big city skyline. When you accordion-fold, your negative space becomes more tall buildings. If you are nervous about cutting into good paper, practice cutting a scrap envelope or some junk mail to warm up. You could use a postcard for reference, or if you live in a city, just look out the window and go!

materials

wide rectangle of grain-short paper
bone folder
good sharp scissors
drawing supplies (markers,
    water-based paint)

optional

collage materials
stickers
rubber stamps

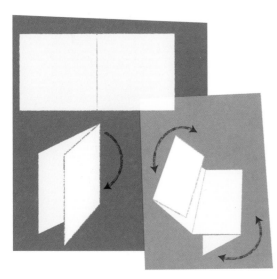

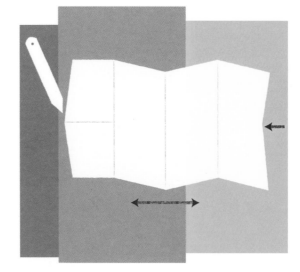

1 Accordion-fold your paper in half along the grain as shown. Always burnish your folds. Fold as many pages as you like.

2 Open paper and fold one end panel in half against the grain. Fold the other end in half just enough to bruise it at the middle, as shown.

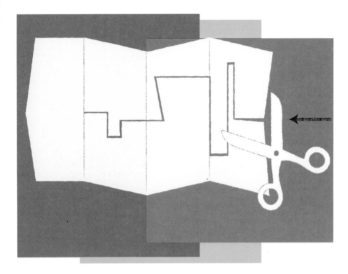 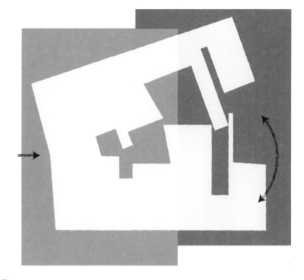

3 Starting at that midpoint, cut a city skyline, being careful not to go too close to the top or bottom (leave at least a quarter of the paper uncut).

4 Cut your skyline until you get to that last folded panel. Stop in the middle, right at that fold.

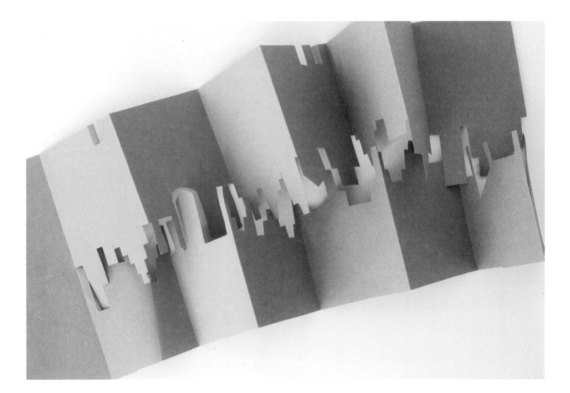

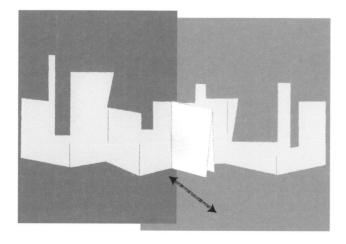

5 Reverse your folds as needed to form an accordion book, as shown.

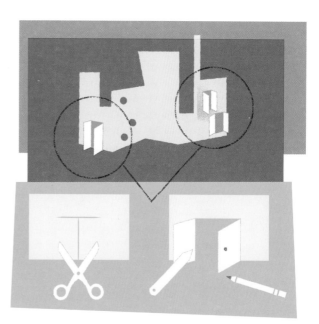

7 You can cut some doorways or windows on the fold.

Tip: You can even add some pop-ups! (See page 58.)

6 Decorate your accordion with drawings and/or collage.

Countryside Accordion

Fold your paper so that it is long and wide instead of tall. Cut rolling hills and mountains instead of a skyline. Draw field animals, barns, trees, etc.

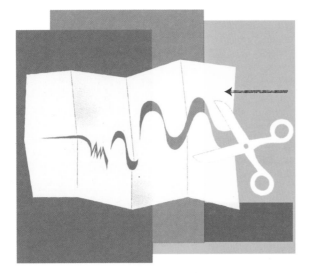

Undersea Accordion

Cut waves instead, and draw fishes and divers and seaweed and sunken treasure.

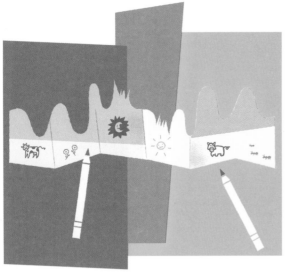

Wellfleet Accordion

Cut scalloped waves as shown—the negative space will be sand dunes. Draw ocean stuff in the ocean and beach stuff on the dunes.

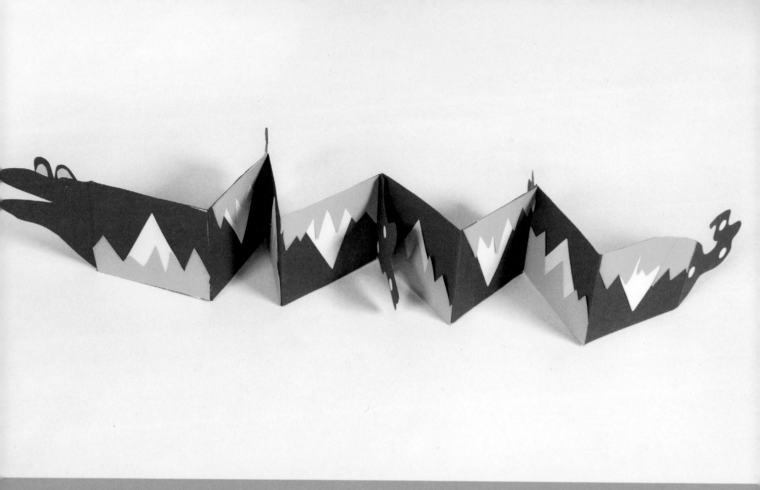

Snaky Salamander Book

This is a version of what I call instant accordion—and I just found out that my colleague, Scott McCarney, invented it. I learned it from one of my students when we were teaching a workshop at Harvard. Ten-year-old Lila Stevens and her mother, Abby Schoolman, a rare book dealer, came down to make books with me. Making this form into a snake was Lila's idea. She made the green one on page 37.

materials

paper
bone folder
glue
scissors
drawing/collage supplies

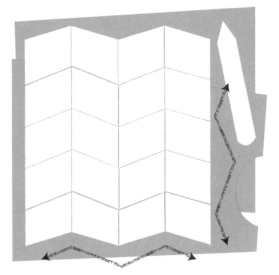

1 Fold your paper in quarters in both directions. Burnish the folds with your bone folder. When you unfold, you will have four panels going across and four panels going down.

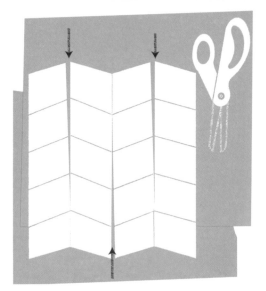

2 Cut into the three interior folds as shown. Make your first cut in the top horizontal fold, cutting from left to right, leaving the last panel intact. On the second horizontal fold, cut from right to left, opposite way from the top fold, leaving that last left-hand panel intact. On the third fold, cut left to right, so that it matches what you did for the first fold.

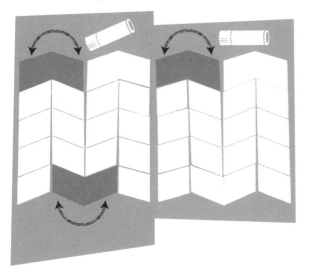

3 Accordion-fold across, starting at the top-left corner, then folding around the intact panels, and back the other way until the whole piece is all folded. Reverse folds as needed.

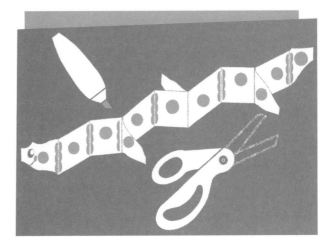

5 When your book is dry, cut into your glued pieces to make designs. Cut the first and last panel to make your head and tail.

6 Finish your book with drawings and/or collage.

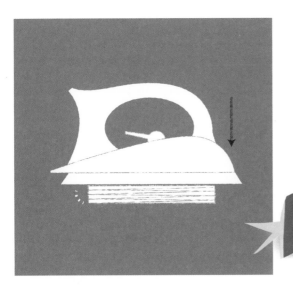

4 Glue your folds together where you turned the corner and left the folds intact as shown in step 3. Burnish and let dry under weight.

Dog & Star-Hinged Accordion

Since no paper comes really, really, really long, you need to come up with ways to make yours long enough—one method is hinging with another piece of paper. You can make these hinges subtle, so they almost disappear. Or have fun with them— show them off and make them the star of your book. Hmm. Speaking of stars!

materials

paper (one color for pages, another color,
    if you like, for hinges)
bone folder
scissors
glue sticks or double-stick tape
drawing and/or collage materials

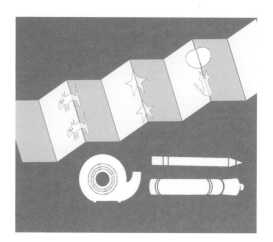

1 Fold several sheets of paper in half. Fold along the grain, not against it.

2 Also paying attention to grain, draw shapes or animals on your contrasting paper. Cut them out and fold them in half—dogs and cats and stars and suns can work for these decorative hinges.

3 Lining up your pages on their base, hold them so that the fore edges meet. Glue your shapes around the fore edges of your pages, a bit up from the bottom and a bit down from the top, to attach your pages together.

4 Now you could collage and/or draw pictures for your book if you like. But your crazy hinges may be all the decoration you need. The front and back pages may be enough for you. Or you can glue on covers (see page 100). Draw and/or collage your covers if your book needs more decoration.

Self-Hinged Accordion Books

To make accordion books, you need to fold along the paper's grain. Ideally your paper will be a very wide strip of short-grain paper. If your paper is not long enough, you can add more pages by hinging.

materials

several sheets of paper, grain short
bone folder
gluestick or double-stick tape
flat book weights (page 22)

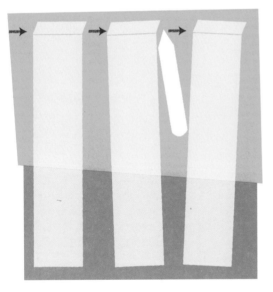

1 Determine the grain of your paper (see page 13). Cut or fold and tear your paper into strips that are the same height as the book you want to make. Try this out with basic copy paper.

2 To make the hinge, fold the end of one of your strips about a thumb's width along the grain. Burnish your fold with your bone folder. Now do this for the other strips.

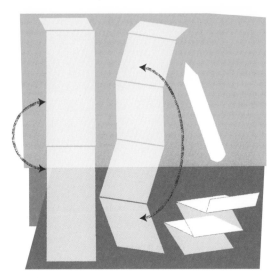

3 Fold one of the strips in half. Make sure the strip is even along the bottom. Fold each half in half again. Keep folding in half until you like the size of your pages, reversing your folds as necessary.

Repeat this with enough paper to make all the pages for your book.

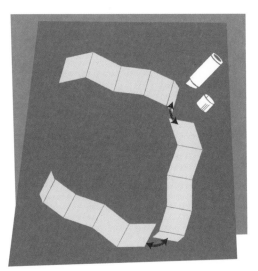

4 When all your pages are folded, paste, glue, or double-stick tape them together attaching the hinge to the next section, as shown, burnishing well.

5 Reverse your folds as necessary so that your accordion lines up and closes.

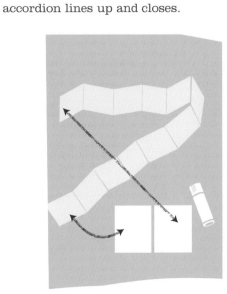

6 Glue covers to the front and back of your accordion (see page 100).

7 Now draw in your book! What will you draw? A picture of your dog or cat or teddy bear or pet octopus?

Accordion Cutout Shape Book

I learned to cut out accordions of people holding hands when I was a child. Michael Bartalos did not do that when he was little, so I showed him how when we were beginning a collaboration, and we made the Purgatory Pie Press limited edition artist book, *Vishnu Crew Stews Vindaloo Anew*. After we designed it, we die-cut paper and aluminum and steel. I asked Michael and his son Bruno to contribute to *Making Books with Kids*. And they made this book of stars. You could try this—or make any shape you like.

materials

a long strip of paper—grain short, easy
  to fold and cut but strong enough to
  stand up
bone folder or spoon for burnishing folds
  and glued covers
pencil
good, sharp scissors
drawing/collage supplies
heavier paper or light board—big enough
  for both front and back covers (upcycle
  a cereal or cracker box)
glue stick, paste, and/or double-stick tape

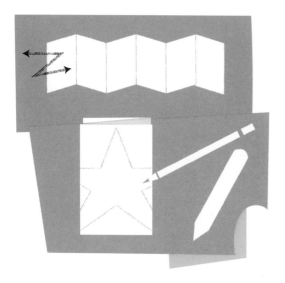

1 Accordion-fold a long piece of grain-short paper. Burnish your folds as usual. If your paper is not long enough, you can hinge your accordion (see page 40).

2 Lightly sketch a shape that meets on the folds.

3 Cut out your shape, being careful to leave the folds intact.

4 Unfold your accordion.

5 Draw and collage if you want to add details.

6 Make two covers by tracing your shape onto the heavier paper or a light board. Cut it out just a touch larger than your shaped accordion book.

8 Decorate your covers with drawings, paint, collage, etc. Protect the inside of the book, wrapping it in waste paper, if you are doing something messy on the cover.

7 Glue the covers to your book on both the front and the back. Always burnish after glueing. Let it dry under a weight (page 22).

Time-Line Accordion Book of ME

My daughter's sixth-grade history teacher asked the class to make a timeline with a photo for every year of their lives. They were supposed to glue photos on a long piece of paper. But I thought an accordion book would be much easier to transport on her school bus—and better protection for the photos too.

Later, I saw an accordion book with one hundred numbered pages in an art exhibit. Each page had a photo of a person whose age matched the page number. It showed all different people—from different places, with different skin tones, dressed in clothing from different cultures—but you could see the progression from baby to teen to adult to parent to grandparent to great-great-grandparent to one of the oldest people in the world in that spread-out accordion in the exhibit case.

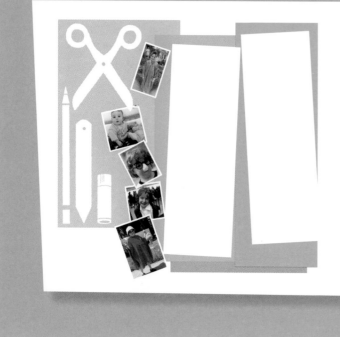

materials

pencil and sketch book or scrap paper for planning
photos, one for each year of your life
cover-weight paper, grain short
bone folder
glue stick or double-stick tape or paste and glue
  with brush
scissors
photo corners or X-Acto knife or box cutter
nonsmear drawing materials to write numbers

optional

corner rounder
light board (you can upcycle a cereal box)

1 Design and plan! You need to organize to make this book. I always sketch in a notebook to work out details. How big is the paper? How big are your photos? What size photos work with the paper? You need to design your book so that each page will be bigger than your photos on all sides.

You can print your digital photos so that they are all the same size. Or if you are using already-printed pictures, pile up your photos. Are they are different sizes? If they are, the largest photo determines your page size.

Take your largest photo and add some space around all sides. How much space? It's up to you. What do you think looks good? You can place your photo on a piece of plain paper and fold back the paper at different widths to see what borders looks most interesting.

2 Plan one page per photo. If the child is ten, you need ten pages. If the child is six, you need six pages. If you want more than one photo per year, add more pages.

When I am planning books, I sketch in a notebook or on scrap paper to figure how my pages will fit onto my paper and how much paper to buy.

Your first photo can be the cover—or you can make a different cover. Or just put your name on the cover. Or put your name and your favorite picture on the cover. Or whatever you like. You are the designer. How does that fit onto your paper?

3 Accordion-fold pages and make your hinges (see page 40 for hinged accordion directions). Burnish the folds with your bone folder.

5 Place your photos on the pages.

6 Mark with your bone folder where the corners will be.

7 Place photo corners or slice diagonally with an X-Acto knife or box cutter. This part is for grownups—and grownups must be careful with the knife!

Then insert photos, one for each year.

Or just glue on your pictures—you can even collage on and around them.

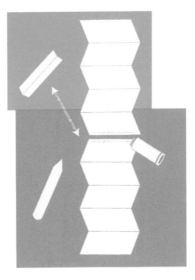

8 Write numbers below, telling the age for each picture. You can make your numbers very fancy and interesting.

4 Glue your hinges, lining up the pages at the bottom so your accordion can stand.

Round the corners with a corner rounder if you like.

Variations

You can even go by fractions instead of whole years—show yourself the day you were born, then six months (half a year, a year), etc., if you like.

My friend made one of these with 12 pages for her baby—a picture from every month of the first year. She planned it on her computer and printed it out in strips so that she could accordion-fold and send as invitations for the baby's first birthday.

You could make this book for an older person. Or one for every year of someone's marriage—or for a holiday or reunion where everyone gets together and takes pictures year after year. When you look at the oldest picture, it's interesting to see what they used to wear. Think about how your pictures will look to people in the future.

9 Decide what to put on the cover. You can let the first page be your cover or glue on a light board cover. You can put a photo on the cover. Or your cover could be your name and your favorite photo. Or you can draw a picture. Or decorate with collage.

Jungle Book Peek-a-Boo

Susan Happerset and I like to make books together, and we also like to go see art exhibits. We saw an interesting accordion catalog at a gallery with text on one layer and pictures on another layer. She played with that idea, and we made this jungle book. She found nice colors of scrapbook paper, so that's what we used— but try this with anything you have handy.

materials

letter-size paper, grain short—use
   contrasting colors or a light-colored
   paper drawing paper
scissors
bone folder
double-stick tape or glue
drawing and collage supplies

1 Cut a strip of paper about half as tall as it
is wide.

2 Cut another strip, about three-fingers-width
shorter on the long ends than you first piece
of paper but the same height.

3 Accordion-fold both sheets into quarters. Use
your bone folder to burnish your folds as usual.

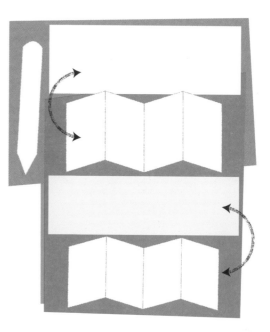

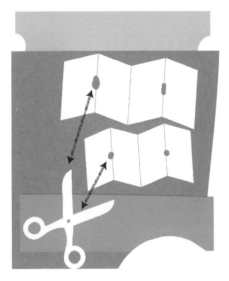

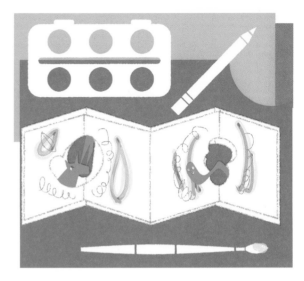

4 Cut a small hole into both valley folds of the larger piece.

5 Cut a smaller hole into both valley folds of the smaller piece.

7 Collage small shapes onto your two pages—use the negative shapes from your cutouts if they look good. You can cut shapes from another contrasting color. Place the collage so that it does not get in the way of your folds.

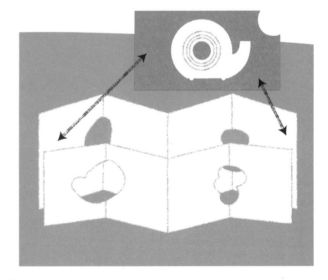

6 Place the smaller accordion into the larger accordion and look at how the holes line up and interact with each other. Adjust your holes, cutting more if you like.

8 Tape or glue (with just a little line of glue) the outer edges together, placing the smaller accordion into the larger accordion.

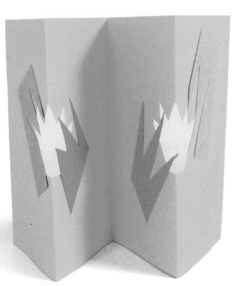

9 Decorate the back too with more cutouts. And/or draw on either or both sides with markers.

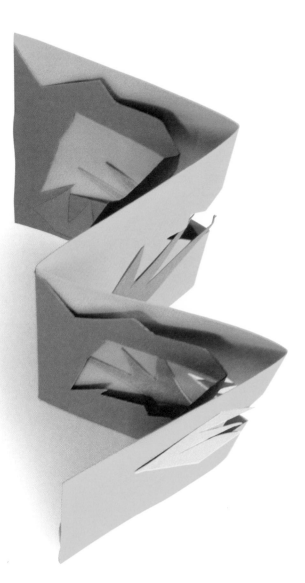

NOTE: Susan Happersett and I cut jungle foliage, but you could also cut out animals or make this into an undersea scene with fish and seaweed and corals. You could also cut the tops of the accordions into a fun shape—the bottoms need to stay even so that your book will stand. You could make another version of this book with translucent paper.

Inside-Outside Book

Jennifer Verbit works with kids in libraries and after-school programs. She always has them make this cut-and-slit book. I had learned this form years ago—so trying it again was like meeting an old friend. A large group of kids in Jennifer's library workshop turned this book into cookbooks. Other kids pasted on faces from the cut scraps. What will you do with yours?

materials

4 sheets of medium-thick paper (like Tru-Ray) that's easy to cut and fold, in two contrasting colors (see page 12 for more on paper)
pushpins
good, sharp scissors
bone folder

optional

drawing and/or collage supplies
glue

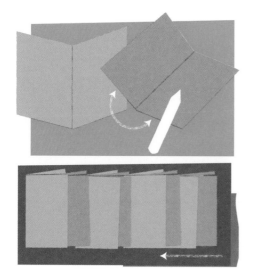

1 Stack two sheets of paper together and fold into signatures. Make two contrasting color signatures of at least two pages each. Burnish the folds with your bone folder.

2 For each sheet of paper, use a pushpin to mark the spines, about a quarter of the way from the top and from the bottom. Also mark the tops so you remember which way is up.

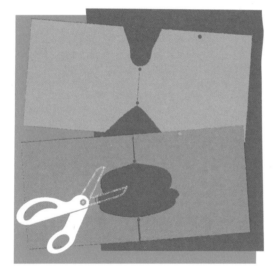

3 Starting and ending at those marks you just made, cut one signature with an inside shape like the one in the picture.

4 Cut the other signature from those same marks with an outside shape similar to the one shown.

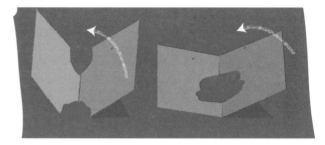

5 Unfold both signatures, keeping their pages together.

6 Roll the signature with the outside shape and hold it like a hotdog bun.

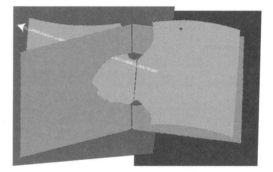

7 Thread this outer signature through the inside shape of the other signature until the folds line up as shown. Be sure the tops you marked are both at the top.

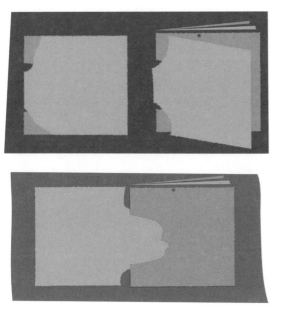

9 Turn the pages of your book around until you see one that looks nice for the cover.

10 Turn the pages to see what your shapes suggest. Maybe your book looks perfect. Or you can draw, write, and glue on the negative shapes to make your book more interesting.

8 Finagle until you can fold the two pieces together in one interlocked section.

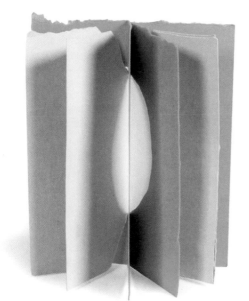

3 making POP-UPS

Pop-ups are the special effects of books—and these easy symmetrical pop-ups give you big bang for your buck. Use them as building blocks—starting very simple, learning the mechanics and letting your kids draw what they imagine. Keep scraps of sturdy, foldable paper for experimenting—and your child will learn to engineer flat paper into active 3-D. Colette Fu's cut-and-assemble photo pop-ups at the end of the chapter show a whole other technique.

At a December workshop at a community center in Harlem, I demonstrated the basic box and asked, "What could this be?"

I thought, "A gift."

But one child said, "A village!" And, working with great concentration, from those simplest boxes she drew a whole scene, with houses and snow and a dark blue sky full of silver sticker stars. Other children went to work, following her example. When they started adding pine trees, I showed them how to make narrow box bases to support glued-on shapes. So many possibilities from the simplest things!

A younger child in that workshop cut and folded pop-up beaks, drew some crazy animals, put them together, and stuck on a cover. He made a book. It was crooked—but such a great, fast first book. What power. Imagine being six, and being able to make your own pop-up book. I wish I'd known how.

Face Pop-Up

Designer Jean Kropper grew up all over the world, but she has lived and worked for most of her adult life in Australia. She made a business card from a little book with this very easy pop-up. I thought you would like making this project based on her idea.

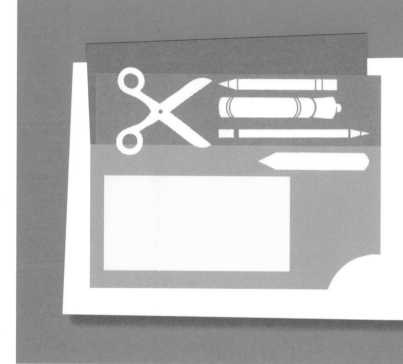

materials

a strip of 90-lb (244 gsm) short-grain
   cover paper (light board or card
   stock) 3 times as long as it is wide
   (or 4 times as long for easier folding)
bone folder
scissors
drawing and/or collage supplies

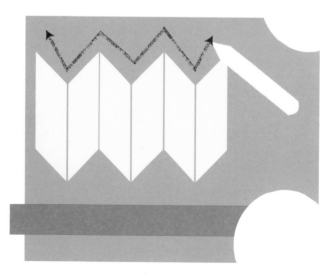

1 Accordion-fold your paper into six or eight even
pages, depending on the size of your strip of paper.
Burnish as usual.

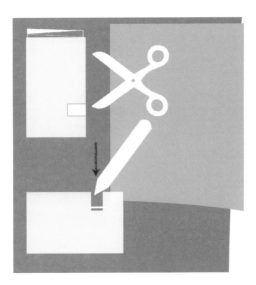

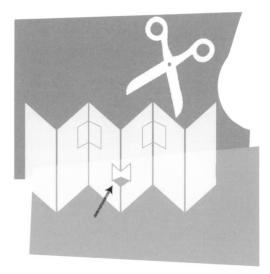

4 Turn your accordion over and fold your pages to expose the mountain folds on either side of that center mouth. Then, toward the top, sketch two more lines that are a bit shallower and closer together than your mouth cuts. These will be the eyes. Cut these slits, then fold and burnish.

2 Open your accordion and, following the folds you just made, fold your whole strip in half.

3 A bit up from the bottom, cut two slits a little less than halfway across that center spread. Fold the inside of this cut and burnish with the bone folder. This is your mouth and nose.

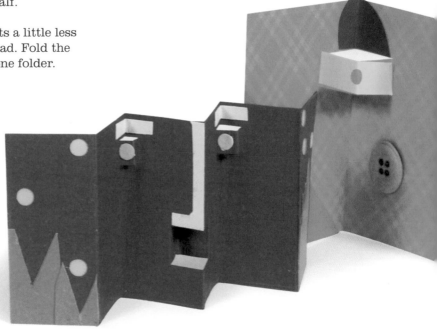

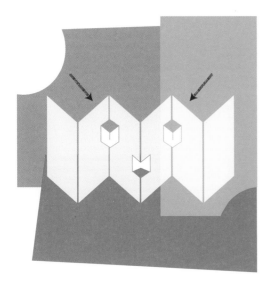

5 Hold your accordion pages like a tent and support with your fingers. Pop the eyes up and the mouth/nose cuts down.

6 Draw and/or collage the eyes, nose, and mouth.

7 If you made the six-fold version, finish the rest of your book. You could draw or collage on the back of your accordion. See what those pop-ups suggest to you and draw that–another face? A house with a door and windows? Or??

8 If you chose the eight-fold version, glue your outside pages back for sturdier covers.

Pop-Up Beaks & Birds & Beasts Book

The beak pop-up can take some practice to fold (its diagonal is against the grain), but it's easy once you practice a few times. And when kids start to draw on them—what fun! You could play with a few for practice before you start the whole book, or make extra pages and choose the ones you love most.

materials

5–6 sheets of 90 lb (244 gsm) cover-weight paper (thick paper that folds well), grain short and approximately letter size to make the pop-ups and another sheet in a contrasting color to make the spine
bone folder
scissors
markers or water-based paint
scrap paper
A piece of heavy-weight paper to cut for the cover
glue and/or double-stick tape

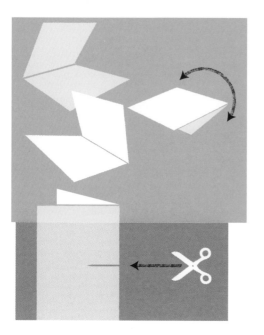

1 Fold your paper in half the short way. Burnish with your bone folder. Reverse this fold and burnish again so that it folds back and forth, loosy-goosey. This will be helpful when you pop your pop-ups. Cut one perpendicular cut straight into the fold as shown.

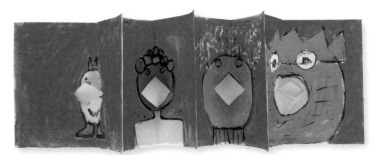

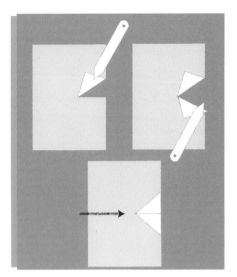

2 Fold top and bottom triangles. Burnish. Reverse the folds and burnish on the other side. Unfold.

4 Draw or paint your bird or beast around the pop-up mouth. You can draw/paint the inside in case it shows when it moves. If you use paint, brush on a thin coat so that it does not crack or clog the mechanism.

5 Cut slits at the same place on all the folded sheets of paper—the slits can be longer or shorter. Pop up those mouths. Draw different animals and birds on the different pages.

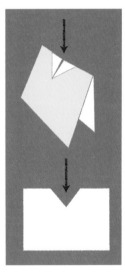

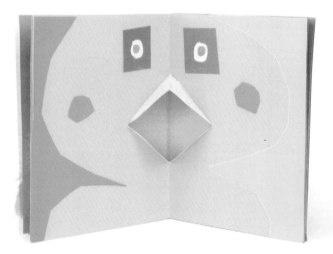

3 Open your paper into a tent shape. Support the paper and push down the triangle folds.

Open and shut your folded paper. The mouth will move. Shut the paper and burnish from the outside.

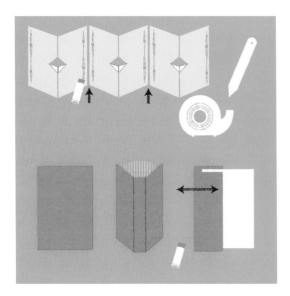

Make Your Cover

7 Fold a piece of scrap paper lightly around the spine to figure out spine thickness. Using that as a template, fold your spine paper with the grain. The spine piece needs to extend past the pop-ups, since it will show when they pop. Glue your spine piece front and back. Avoid gluing to the spine so it can move when you open your book.

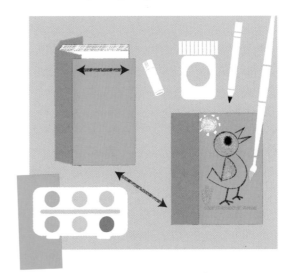

6 Glue your pop-up pages together at their fore edges. Burnish well with your bone folder.

8 Cut the contrasting pieces of heavy paper or light board to fit the front and back. These covers can be a bit taller than your book or the same height. They should be narrower than your book to allow the spine piece to show.

9 Glue the covers in place on the front and back of your book. Burnish well. Open with great care. Check that nothing that needs to move is sticking. Let rest under a weight (see page 22) for as long as you can stand not playing with it.

Ice Cream Cone Pop-Up

Colette Fu lives in Philadelphia—one of the Great American Ice Cream Cities. My mother grew up there. She told me stories of going to the Reading Terminal when she was a child and eating lunch backwards—ice cream first! You can make copies of this for practice before you do the real one. After you understand how this works, you can make your own versions of this pop-up.

materials

Ice Cream Cone Pop-Up pages
    See pages 71–74, or download
    at www.quartoknows.com/page/
    making-books
scissors
bone folder
glue

optional

light card stock

1 Cut out the Ice Cream Cone Pop-Up pages from the book. Or photocopy, scan, or download and print the pages onto light card stock.

2 Valley-fold the background in half so that the sky and gray areas are on the inside of your paper, and burnish.

3 Cut out the ice cream cone

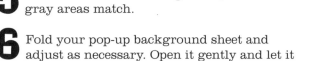

5 Glue the tabs to the background, so that the gray areas match.

6 Fold your pop-up background sheet and adjust as necessary. Open it gently and let it dry before you play.

4 Mountain-fold the ice cream cone in half, following the vertical dotted line. Mountain-fold the tabs on the dotted lines. Burnish these folds with your bone folder.

7 Yum!

Cut & Assemble Pop-Ups

Ice Cream Cone Pop-Up: This is the other side of the cone.

Inside cover Ice Cream Cone Pop-Up. Directions page 68.

CUT and POPPED by: ....

Ice Cream Cone Pop-Up cover. Instructions page 68.

Cut, colored and popped by:

Jane's Spinning Flower Pop-Up variation, inside cover. Directions page 83.

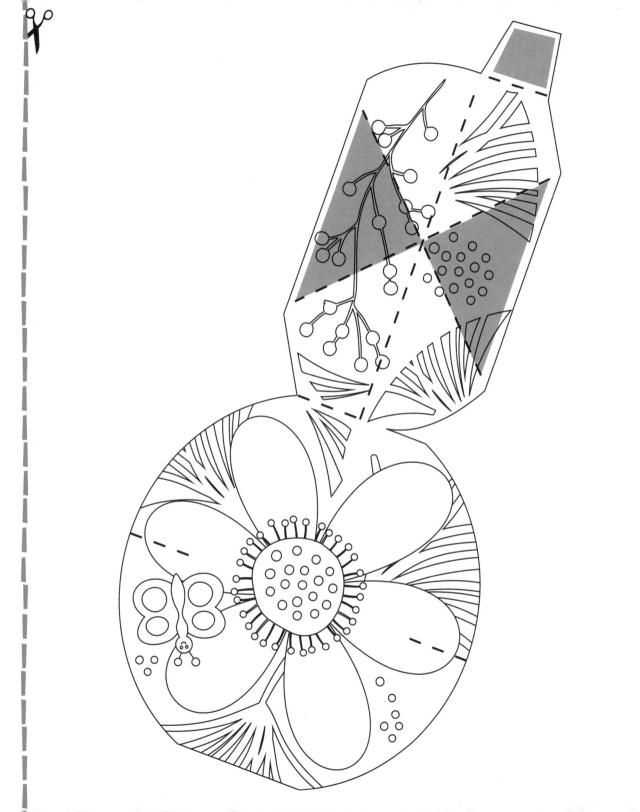

Jane's **Spinning Flower** variation for you to cut, fold, color, and glue to its cover, opposite. Directions page 83.

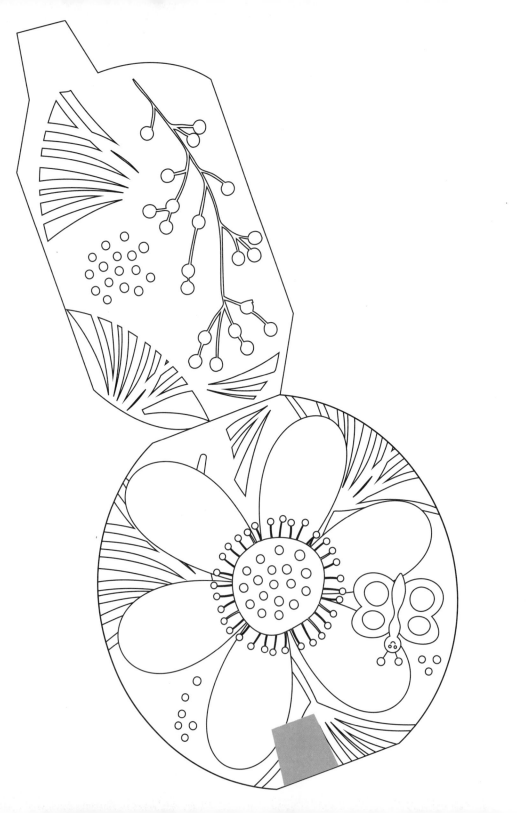

Spinning Flower Pop-Up variation you can color. This is the backside of the pop-up flower.

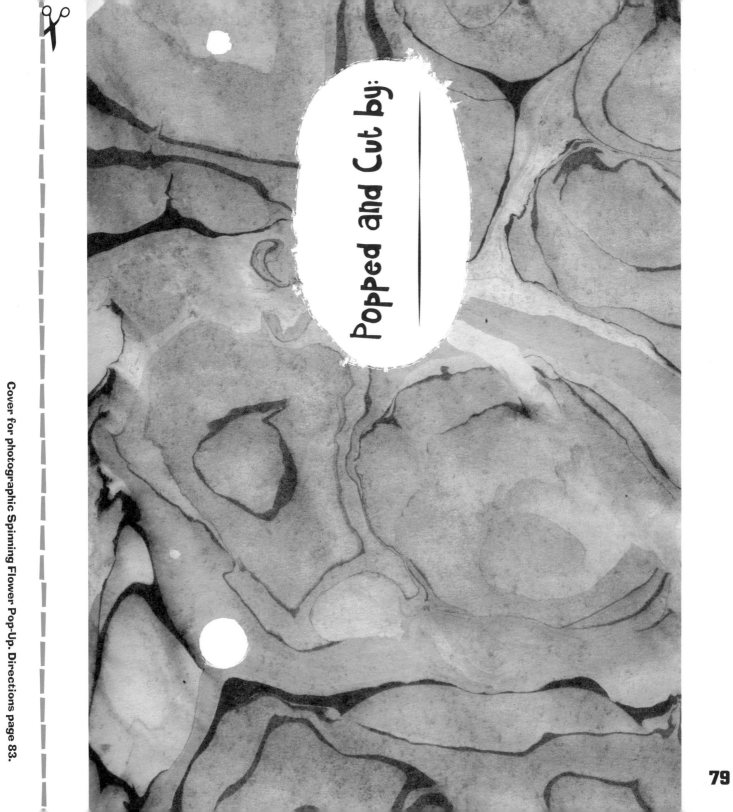

Popped and Cut by: _____

Colette Fu's photographic Spinning Flower Pop-Up inside cover. Directions page 83.

81

Colette's **Spinning Flower back**

Spinning Flower Pop-Up

Colette Fu is a photographer who learned pop-ups to make her photos come alive. She travels to China and takes pictures of people and plants and food. She makes books with her pop-ups that look simple and elegant and then open very tall and wide. She shows these books in exhibitions. Some museums collect Colette's books.

This pop-up is tricky. But it is worth the practice to learn to pirouette paper. Make some copies to try first. Once you understand the paper engineering, try your own design. Note: The mechanism is the same width as the flower.

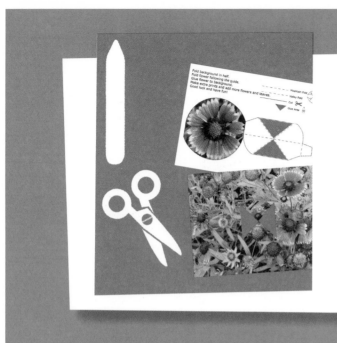

materials

Spinning Flower Pop-Up pages
  (see pages 79-82)
Several printouts of the flower and cover for
  practice (download at www.quartoknows.com/
  page/making-books).
scissors
bone folder
glue

Note: pages 75-78 have the version that Jane
Sanders drew. Make that one, too.

1 Cut out the Spinning Flower Pop-Up pages from the book. Or download (www.quartoknows.com/page/making-books) and print the Spinning Flower Pop-Up pages onto a light card stock.

2 Fold the background in half so that the gray triangles are on the inside. Burnish your folds.

3 Cut out the flower and its attached mechanism.

4 Mountain-fold the flower in half, following the vertical blue dotted lines. The dotted lines do not go all the way through the flower, but your fold should.

5 Mountain-fold between the flower and the mechanism on the dotted blue line. Mountain-fold the x's dotted blue lines on the mechanism. Mountain-fold the tab on the dotted blue line.

6 Valley-fold along the dotted red horizontal line. Burnish all these folds with your bone folder.

7 Glue the mechanism to the background at the gray triangles.

8 Fold your flower into its mechanism and glue the tab to the back of the flower.

9 Fold your pop-up background sheet with great care and adjust as necessary. Open it and let it dry before you play with it.

10 And, as Colette says, "Have fun!"

Kids made these popups.

Lots of kids helped me with this book. Some of them grew up before I wrote it—but they inspired me to tell the publisher that I wanted to write **MAKING BOOKS WITH KIDS**. Some kids came over and cut and folded and popped and drew, sitting around my big yellow table.

We always started by baking scones that we invented—but that's a story for another book! Other kids made things at my book store events at McNally Jackson in New York City and Jersey City **WORD**. Liz Grace, an artist who teaches after school in Connecticut, took the train down. And before we went to Chinatown for soup dumplings, I showed her how to make some books and simple pop-ups. She went back and worked with her students and brought me their work.

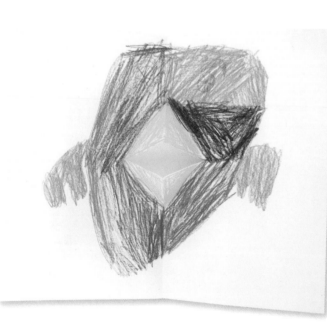

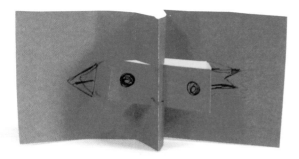

Now that you know some basic pop-ups, what will you make? You are on your way to Paper Engineering. (And building bridges could be the next step after that.)

4 Decorating PAPERS

Some people love painting papers. When I did this with a group of adult students, I saw them relax as they spread the color with their brushes.

Be careful to keep your paint layers thin, so the finished sheets can fold without cracking. This may be tricky for children. But you can give them extra paper for making pictures.

Plan to paint papers a day or two before you make books so that there is plenty of drying time. Or do it early in the morning, knowing you will work with your decorated paper late in the afternoon if it has dried enough. Humidity is an issue. In New York City—especially in the summer, nothing ever dries. But if you live near a desert, you may not need to wait so long.

Some decorative papers do not look interesting in big sheets, but when you fold them down, they have a nice presence. Once, we ended up with a bunch of abandoned papers from a group of kids. They had mostly just written their names on them. I needed to make a bunch of envelopes for party favors, so I cut them down and folded them—the small pieces of large handwriting looked beautiful out of context.

Soap Bubble Papers

When I was a kid, we always hoped they'd give us straws in restaurants. I did not like milk—I HATED MILK, though now I like it and have to try not to drink too much. What I did love was the bubbles it made when you blew into a glass of milk with a straw. One time we were at a restaurant with my nieces who were around my age (can you believe I was an aunt when I was two?), and we asked for straws. The waiter brought them, but said, "No blowing bubbles." We did not like that. We would have loved making these bubble papers. It's one of the most fun things you can do—and some of your results might look OK too. (Just remember to blow out the straw—don't sip the soap!)

materials

cups
baking sheet (or dish larger than your paper)
water
dishwashing liquid
food color or tempera paints
drinking straw
uncoated paper in white and/or assorted colors and various weights, lighter for endsheets and heavier for covers

1 Place your cup on the baking sheet or dish that is larger than your paper. Combine a little water with a squirt of dishwashing liquid.

2 Add a squirt of food color or water-based paint in your cup.

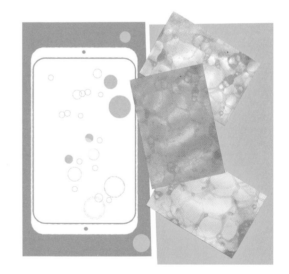

4 Lay your paper in the pan of bubbles, press it a bit, and then remove it. See the print that the bubbles made on your paper.

3 Put your straw in the cup and blow bubbles until they overflow onto the baking sheet.

5 Try some variations with different colors. You can use a few cups with different colors—blow the bubbles onto your baking dish to combine them. Play with this idea and see what variations you can invent. (I wish I could see them!) Let your papers dry.

Salt Papers

Salt is the magic in this easy, fun technique. See how colors break down into other colors. Some of the dullest colors can become the most interesting salt papers!

materials

paper
sponges to dampen paper
water
tempera paint or watercolor (a high-quality
  nonwaxy brand like Prang or Caran d'Ache)
brushes
table salt

1 Dampen your papers with a sponge.

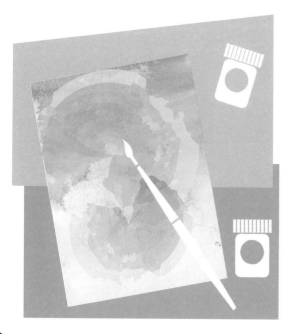

2 Paint the papers with a light coat of watered-diluted tempera paint or watercolor.

3 Sprinkle salt over your paper—watch as the salt changes the colors. (Black breaks down into many different colors.)

Experiment on small pieces of paper with several colors to see what breaks down best. Make larger sheets of your favorites.

4 Let your papers rest for a few hours or overnight. When the paint dries, brush off the salt. Use this paper for book covers and endsheets, or make book pages from it, and write poems and draw pictures into the patterns.

NOTE: You can use these decorated papers for endsheets and/or covers. You can even make books with decorative paper pages and see what its shapes suggest and draw into them. Like looking at the clouds in the sky—maybe you will see animal shapes, or birds, or ships at sea.

Shaving Cream Marbling

Try to find unscented shaving cream, or find a scent that you really, really like! One of my Cooper Union students, who was an elementary school teacher, showed the class this very silly trick. She brought us paper plates to use instead of baking pans—but if you are doing this in a kitchen; a pan may fit your papers better. Your marbled paper is good for book covers, endsheets, covering boards, etc. Let it rest for a bit and then trim it if you need to, so that the most interesting part shows when you use it.

NOTE: Use the weight of paper that works best for your needs. Thinner paper is better for endsheets—or covering boards (see page 100). Cover-weight paper or card stock is better for covers.

materials

foam shaving cream (do not use gel)
cookie sheet or cake pan or paper plates
squeegee or scraper (can be a piece of paper plate)
food coloring or liquid watercolor or tempera or
    watered-down acrylics with droppers
toothpicks or chopsticks for swirling
uncoated papers smaller than the size of your
    plate or pan

1 Spray shaving cream onto your plate or pan.

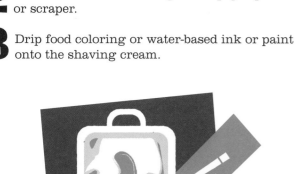

2 Smooth the cream with a piece of paper plate or scraper.

3 Drip food coloring or water-based ink or paint onto the shaving cream.

4 Swirl the color with toothpicks.

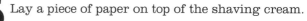

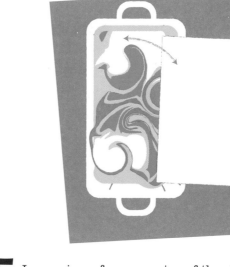

5 Lay a piece of paper on top of the shaving cream.

6 Lift off the paper and scrape away the excess shaving cream—it dries very fast.

7 You can use the shaving cream more than once—add color as needed.

Suminagashi

This is a traditional Japanese paper-decorating technique. It is easy to set up. The resulting papers are pale so you can use them to write and draw on for the interiors of your books—or for endsheets or covers or to cover boards (see page 100).

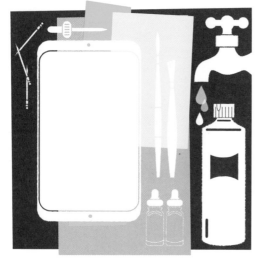

materials

water pans (can be baking pans)
water
water-based inks or paint (or even food coloring)
droppers, brushes, toothpicks
paper that fits in your water pan
light board for skimming excess paint
book weights (see page 22)

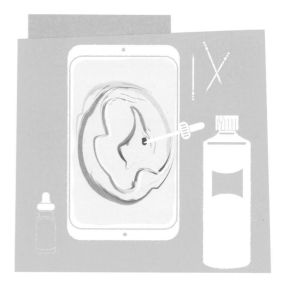

1 Fill your water pan with water. Drip inks into the water.

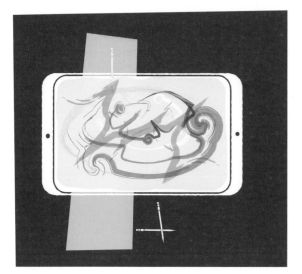

2 You can swirl your inks with toothpicks, or just let them flow.

3 With great care, float your paper on top of the water.

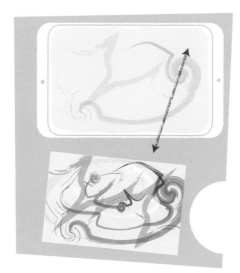

4 Remove the paper with great care. Skim your water to remove paint with the edge of a piece of light board. To decorate more sheets of paper, you can repeat the whole process, starting with dripping your inks.

5 Let your paper dry, and rest it under weights to flatten.

6 Trim and use this paper for book covers and endpapers.

Paste Papers

Paste paper is a traditional method for decorating papers. It may remind you of finger paint—which is based on paste papers. But brush your paste thin so that you can fold your decorative papers and use them for endsheets or for covering boards. You can even paint raw boards with it. We made paste-paper boards using metallics in our paste, and it looked very interesting and a little mysterious.

Dikko made paste papers for the endsheets and flyleaf for this book. He brushed on the red paste and then marked it with a spiral egg whisk to get that design. (Now where did he put our whisk? I need it back in the kitchen.)

materials

1 or 2 cups wheat paste (depending on how many people will be making paste papers; see page 17)
smallish bowls or takeout containers
water-based color (tempera, gouache, acrylic, powder paint, or even food coloring)
sponge
brushes
water
paper
forks, combs, stamps, marking things (you can cut combs from light board or heavy paper—try pieces of a cereal box)
book weights (see page 22)

1 Divide cooled paste into several cups or bowls that will not tip too easily.

2 Add a squirt or two of color to each one—like coloring icing for cake or cookie decoration—and stir.

4 Brush a very thin coat of color paste onto the paper. Keep this thin so that your paper can fold later.

3 Sponge or paint your paper with plain water to dampen.

5 Using forks, etc., scrape designs into your paper.

6 Let your papers dry and then place under weights to flatten (see page 22).

Paste Paper Covers for Accordion Books

You can use paste paper to cover these boards or try marbled papers (pages 94 or 96) or salt papers (page 92) if you like. You can also buy decorative paper or use something interesting you already have—maybe a nice piece of wrapping paper or scrapbook paper. You could also use book cloth from a bookbinding specialty store or even contact paper!

materials

accordion books (page 38, 40, and 46)
board—upcycled cereal/cracker box, or the
    insides from mats (ask your local framer for
    scraps!), or bookbinding board, or museum board
healable cutting mat
pencil
metal straightedge
utility knife, mat knife, heavy-duty paper
    cutter, or very strong, sharp scissors
glue and brush or other adhesive
paste paper (page 98) or other decorative paper
bone folder
waste paper
book weights (page 22)

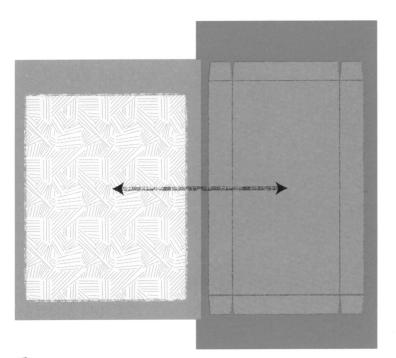

1 Marking the size with your pencil, and using your cutting mat, straightedge, and knife, cut two boards just a hair bigger than the pages of your accordion book.

2 Cut your decorative paper a thumb's width bigger than the boards on all sides.

3 Glue board to the back of your decorative paper. Repeat for other board.

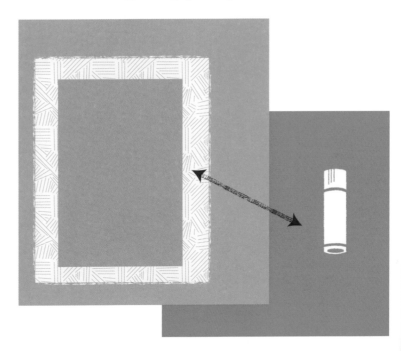

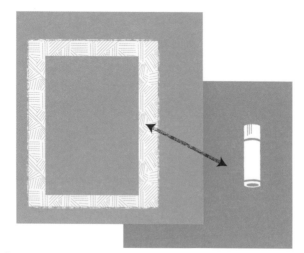

4 Fold the top and bottom over your boards, and burnish with your bone folder. Open, and then fold the sides over boards, burnish, and open again.

5 To remove corner bulk, cut away the paste paper. Hold your straightedge against a corner of the board and trace a diagonal line. Trim away the paper, leaving enough to cover the corners—approximately the thickness of your straightedge. Trim all eight corners of your two boards.

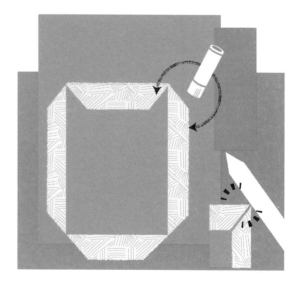

6 Glue the tops and bottoms, gluing out to the edges with waste paper underneath, using as little glue as necessary. Fold the tops and bottoms up over the board, pressing material over the corners, smoothing with your bone folder.

7 Glue the sides. Use your bone folder to press the material in at the corner.

8 Let your covers rest under book weights—you will know they are dry when they are no longer cool to the touch.

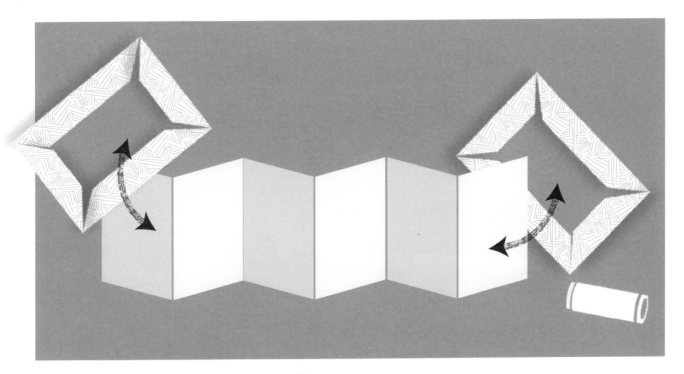

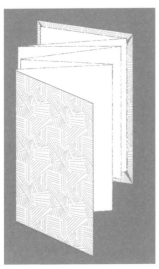

9 Glue the front and back pages of the accordion to your cover. Burnish as usual and rest under a flat book weight.

NOTE: Depending on your accordion, you may want to attach it to covers with a hinge (see page 40). Then you could cover the inside raw board, gluing down an endsheet of the same or contrasting decorative paper. Cut that endsheet just a little smaller than your board.

5 Sewing Books

My aunt taught me to sew when I was six. I made troll doll clothes. (My aunt also said that if I married a man named Mr. Lemonade I would be named Esther Lemonade. Somehow my husband refused to change his name to Lemonade.)

I had mono for four months when I was 10. My mother's friend Diana brought me an embroidery kit. I cross-stitched **HAPPY DAYS MAKE A HAPPY YEAR.** When embroidered jeans got popular a few years later, I was ready. Like embroidery, sewing books is relaxing and meditative.

Let your kids have fun sewing. It's OK if their stitches are uneven. Help them make it work, but don't do it for them. They will learn by doing, and they will do what they enjoy. Let kids invent.

When I showed my helpers, Michael and Mateo, how to stab-stitch flip books, Michael said, "Sewing books is wonderful! There is nothing as satisfying as finishing sewing a book." I too like to sew books. Watching piles of paper become piles of books IS very satisfying.

Tiny Book

This simple sewn pamphlet book is so small that your toy can read it. You may need to make a bunch of them so that the other toys won't be jealous.

materials

thin piece of paper, like copy paper
bone folder
cover-weight paper to fit
scissors for trimming the cover
phone book or thick magazine
awl or pushpins for hole punching
tapestry needle
linen bookbinding thread
drawing supplies (markers, pens) that
    don't smear

1 Fold the thin paper in half and in half again, and again, and again, until it gets very small. Burnish with your bone folder.

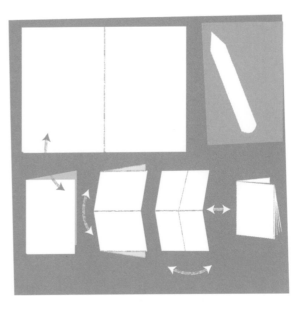

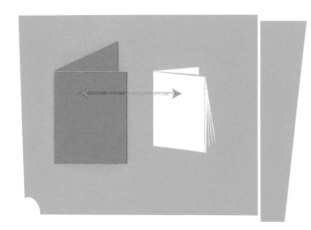

2 Fold a cover to go around the paper. Remember to fold on the grain. Trim to fit.

3 Place the cover-weight paper on an opened phone book, or thick magazine, and then center your folded paper on the cover.

4 Punch three holes—near the top, bottom, and middle—using your awl or a pushpin.

5 Tear or slit the pages with the end of the bone folder (or do this after you stitch).

6 Thread your needle, locking your thread onto the needle (at right).

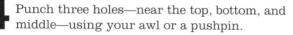

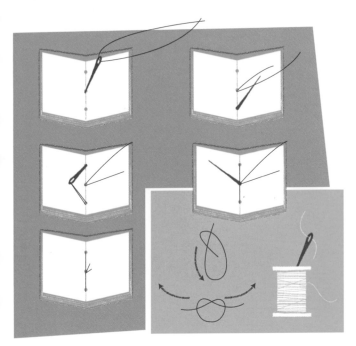

7 Pamphlet stitch: Start in the middle hole, leaving a tail long enough to tie later. Come back into your book via the top or bottom hole. Skip the middle hole. Go through the last hole. Come back through the middle hole—on the other side of your long stitch. Tie the ends over long thread with a square knot (see inset above).

Cut your thread—not too short. Draw pictures and/or write a story of your bear or doll or toy.

NOTE: You can stitch buttons or beads on the spine. Start stitching inside or outside. If you start outside, the tails of your thread can be decorative—you can tie buttons or beads or even small bells on the ends. If you start inside, the thread tails will not show as much.

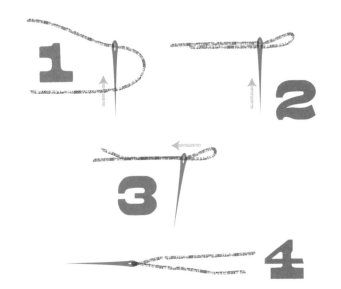

How to Lock Thread onto a Needle for Stitching Ease

1 Thread your needle, leaving a tail of about 3" (7.6 cm).

2 Pierce the tail with the needle, forming a loop.

3 Push the loop down onto the long thread.

4 Tug the long thread to tighten the loop, locking your thread on the needle.

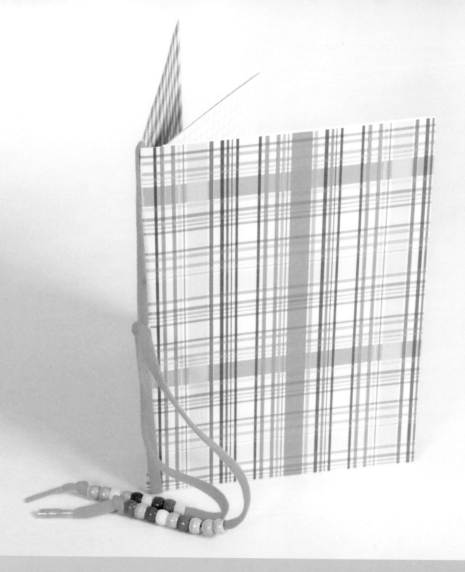

Shoelace Book

A shoelace is like a threaded needle. Only not sharp. When I was a kid, there were sewing cards for girls. Boys were not supposed to learn to sew then—so those boys were stuck if their buttons fell off. Those cards came with shoelaces for stitching. Kids too young for needles—or anyone else, can sew a book with a long shoelace.

materials

paper—light cover stock and
  text-weight papers
bone folder
awl
shoelace three times as long as
  the spine of your book
markers for drawing

optional

beads

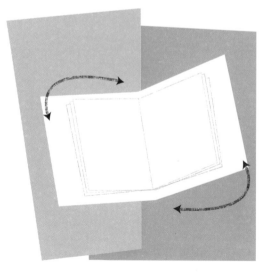

1 Fold a signature and, as usual, burnish with
your bone folder (see page 14 if you need help
with this).

2 Fold a cover around it—have the cover extend
past the fore edge of your signature.

3 Punch a hole in the center with the awl.

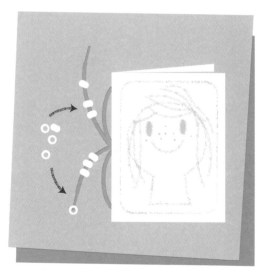

4 From the outside, thread your shoelace through the center hole. Go to the top and pull the shoelace around to the bottom. Bring it up the inside of your book and back out the hole.

5 Place the ends of the shoelace on either side of the long stitch. Tie a square knot, left over right and right over left (see inset on page 109). You can tie a bow over the knot. Add beads if you like.

6 Draw and/or paint pictures in your book. Since it's a shoelace, you could draw pictures of all your sneakers—or all your family's sneakers and their shoestrings.

Rubber Band Notebook

Here is a simplified one-signature book—you do not even need to stitch if you have a rubber band that stretches to the height of your spine.

materials

thin, letter-size paper in assorted colors
bone folder or scissors
heavy, but foldable, cover stock cut to the same height as your folded signature and wide enough to fit around it for your cover
ponytail rubber bands—colors that contrast with your paper

1 Fold the thin paper in half lengthwise and then crosswise. Slit the paper with your bone folder (or scissors) so that you have a folded section with two sheets of paper. This becomes eight pages when you count the fronts and backs. If you want sixteen pages, you can fold and slit another sheet of paper and nestle that inside your first section.

2 Cut the heavyweight piece to the same height and fold it around the lightweight paper to make your cover. It needs to be a little bigger on the fore edge to go around the interior pages. You can have it extend out and then fold back the flaps, or you can use two layers of the card stock to give it enough strength to support the rubber band.

3 Open your signature. Stretch a rubber band around the pages and let it rest on the fold. Close your book and adjust the rubber band so that it lies flat. Vary your paper and rubber band sizes as necessary for this project—and to make smaller and larger notebooks.

4 Tuck your little book into your pocket with a pen for notes and observations. Since it is a rubber band book, you could draw pictures of ponytails and braids.

Felt Needle Book

You can make this book to keep your own bookbinding needles—but it would also be a nice gift for your favorite person who sews. Bookbinder Mindell Dubansky repairs books at the Metropolitan Museum of Art in New York City. She made me a version of this book from brocade upholstery fabric. She fringed the edges, and sewed from the outside, adding beads to her thread. It was so pretty that at first I kept it with my artist books collection. But when I put it in my box of tools and started using it, it became a part of my life. I think of Mindy whenever I sew.

materials

felt—several colors
scissors
needle and linen thread, or awl
   and shoelace
needles to put in your book

optional

buttons and beads for decoration
glue
assorted safety pins
pinking sheers

1 Decide how big you want your book to be. It could be tiny—just big enough for a few needles—or large enough to also store your scissors and bone folder.

2 Cut two to four pieces of felt twice as wide as your final size. Use straight scissors or pinking shears. You can alternate felt colors if you like.

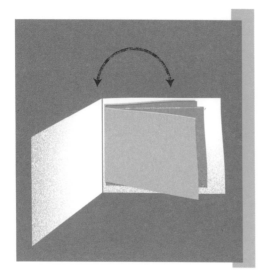

3 Fold your felt pieces in half, and wrap another
piece of felt around to be the cover—the cover can
be the same height or just a touch bigger than your
pages, but will need to be a little wider so that it can
go around the pages without anything sticking out.

5 Decorate your cover with buttons and/or beads
and/or pieces of felt. You can glue them on with
tacky glue, or pin them and stitch with a pretty color
of thread, or use safety pins of assorted sizes to attach
your felt collage as part of the design.

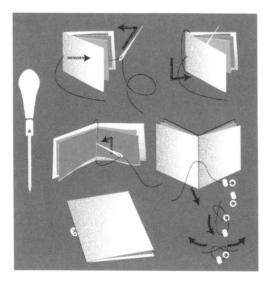

4 Stitch with a pamphlet stitch through the
spine (page 109), or punch holes and stitch
with a shoelace.

6 Stick your needles on the pages in
interesting patterns.

NOTE: If you like to do fancy sewing, you can use scraps of brocade and add trim, like this antique needle book.

Variation

Like Mindy, you can use other fabrics and pull threads on the edges to fringe them—this could be a nice project to do with an old pair of jeans. You could even include the pockets for tools like your bone folder and scissors.

Book Bag Book

Elise Engler has made inventory drawings her whole life. An inventory is like a list—but Elise draws everything on the list. I ran into her when she was drawing every block of Broadway in New York City—and Broadway goes for more than 200 blocks. A few years ago, she did a project where she drew women's purses and their contents. She also drew refrigerators and everything that was in those. When I told her I was writing this book, she suggested kids make a book with everything in their school bags. I liked that idea—and I hope you enjoy her project!

materials

Pencil and paper for sketching
your school bag, with all the stuff inside
paper for the pages of your book
bone folder
cover-weight paper or light board
phone book or thick magazine to use
    as a book cradle
awl or pushpin
needle and thread
drawing supplies that will not smear
good, sharp scissors

optional

shoelace
glue, paste, glue stick, or double-stick tape

1 Sketch your book bag.
How is your book bag shaped
like a book? Does it have straight sides?
How will it fit on a rectangle?

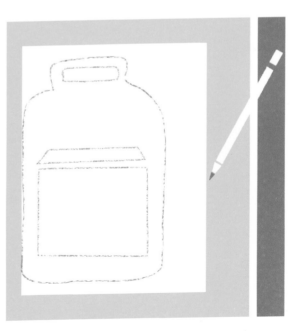

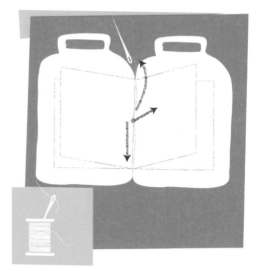

2 Plan your pamphlet book so that the cover is shaped like the bag—but so that one side or one end is flat, to fit on your fold. Your inside signature can be rectangular. It needs to be a little smaller than your cover so that the pages do not stick out.

4 Pamphlet-stitch your book (page 109) with needle and thread—or make larger holes and pamphlet stitch with a shoelace (page 112).

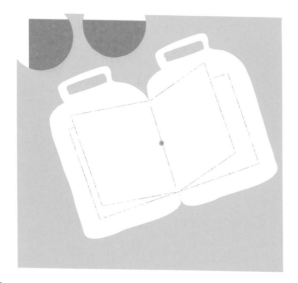

3 Lay your open signature in your open cover, resting on your book cradle. Punch stitching holes with your awl.

5 Empty your book bag and line everything up on your table.

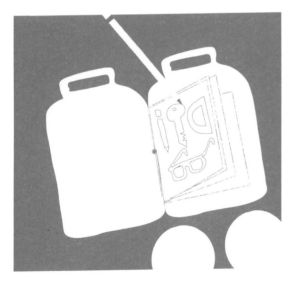

6 Draw everything in your bag on the pages of your book.

Variations

You can stitch a simple, rectangular pamphlet book about the same proportion as the book bag. Then draw your book bag shape a little bigger than your pages. Cut it out and glue it to the cover. You need to leave a little space at the spine so that it opens without "binding."

Or just draw your book bag on the book cover and the contents inside.

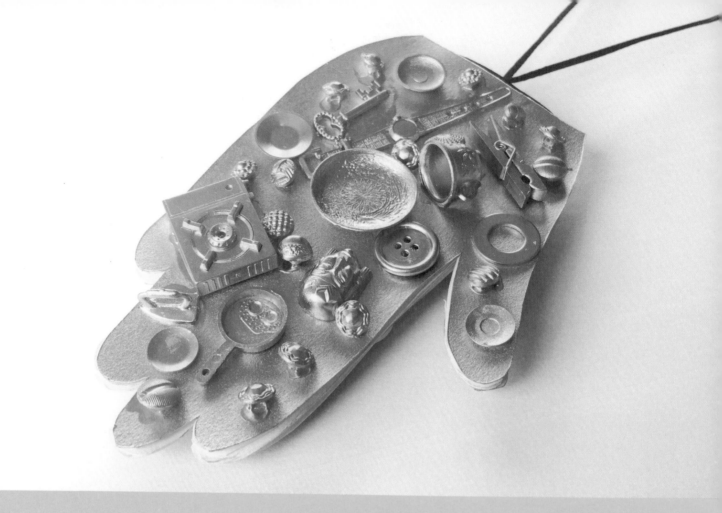

Three Wishes Amulet Book

Artist Miriam Schaer loves to travel, and she stitches hand books from newspapers when she goes to countries with different writing systems. She has also made sculptural artist's books from unusual materials—sometimes starting by painting a dress with acrylic medium and then embedding a book. She has done this with doll clothes and baby clothes. She has even made huge book sculptures with wedding dresses.

materials

pencil
scissors
paper for interior
bone folder
hole punch
shoelace, ribbon, or string—the length should measure
    from the width of your shoulder to the fingertips of
    your opposite outstretched arm
collage and/or drawing supplies for interior
light board for cover (can be a cereal box)
glue
collage material for your cover (can be buttons and other
    dimensional, nonporous objects, including tacky glue)
waxed paper
soft book weight (page 22)

optional

paint (can be spray-paint)

1 Trace your closed hand on a piece of paper and
cut out the pattern.

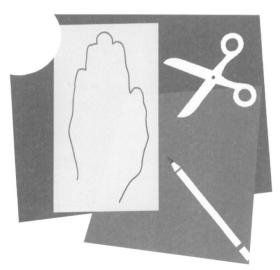

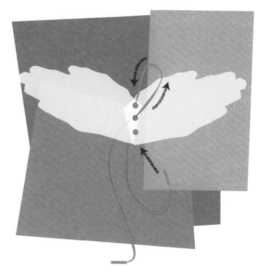

2 Fold a signature of three sheets of your interior paper along the grain. Trace your pattern so that the bottom of the hand or wrist is on the fold.

3 Cut out the shape, leaving your fold intact.

5 Pamphlet stitch starting outside of the spine at the middle hole, leaving a long tail (as shown).

6 Tie your square knot around the stitch on the outside center. Then tie the two long tails together at the ends with an overhand knot (looping the two ends together, inserting the tail and pulling through the loop) so that you can slip it over your head.

4 Punch three holes on your fold—one in the middle and one about a finger's width from each end.

7 Draw and/or collage your three wishes inside your book—one wish for yourself, one wish for your family, and the third wish for the world.

Cover

8 Trace your pattern onto the light board and cut the covers out—they should be a hair bigger than the signature, but flush at the wrist, one turned opposite from the other, if your board is one-sided (like a cereal box).

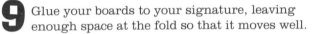

9 Glue your boards to your signature, leaving enough space at the fold so that it moves well.

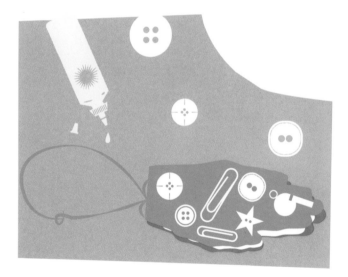

10 Embellish your boards with collage and/or drawings. You can use tacky glue to attach nonporous things like buttons and tiny toys.

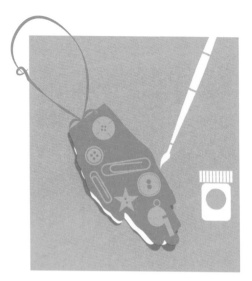

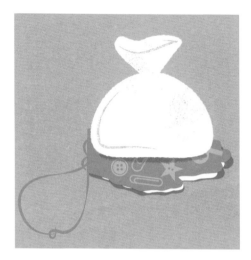

11 If your collage had dimensional textures, you could paint the boards à la Louise Nevelson. Gold spray-paint can work for that—but use it outdoors. When I lived in my old apartment, I would open the window to spray-paint things on my fire escape. That does not work where I live now, but I sometimes take things outdoors to paint. Or you could paint with acrylic, which would be a little goopy—but that would add more texture.

If you are painting your covers, wrap the book with waxed paper or something to protect it from the cover paint.

12 Protect your book with waxed paper and weight down with soft weights—like a bag of rice or split peas—or a weight you have sewn (see p.22)

13 Let everything dry as long as you can before you wear your amulet to bring luck to you and your family and your world. If you are gluing on small pieces of plastic, let it dry under a weight for a few days. Don't be shocked if something falls off—just put it in your pocket and fix it later—you might even improve your original design.

Paper Hand Book Variation

We made a simpler version of this hand book.

1 Follow steps 1-3 for the Amulet Book.

2 Fold your cover paper around the signature—it needs to be a little larger to cover—and trim the hand a bit larger than your inside paper.

3 Punch a hole in the center of the fold.

4 Pamphlet stitch with the shoelace starting outside of the spine at the middle hole, leaving a long tail (as shown.) Adjust the shoelace so that both ends are even. Tie your square knot around the middle string close to the book.

5 Tie the ends together in an overhand knot, so that it fits over your head. Or leave ends loose so that you can tie them when you put on your amulet.

6 Decorate your cover. Inside your book draw or collage three wishes—one for yourself, one for your family, and one for the world.

materials

pencil
paper
scissors
bone folder
glue stick

cover paper
collage and/or drawing
    materials
hole punch
long shoelace

127

Juggling Balls Flip Book

Draw with a hole punch on two or three colors of bright paper to make this quick, fun flip book. Practice punching holes on scraps before you design your book to see how far your hole puncher will let you punch. Note: Awls are sharp—don't poke your eye out!

materials

10-plus pieces of approximately 90-lb (244 gsm) cover-weight paper or cardstock, approximately 3" x 6" (8 x 15 cm), grain short, in 2 or more contrasting colors
pencil
bone folder
cup for tracing
hole punch
thick rubber band and binder clips
awl
tapestry needle
3-ply linen thread or hole punch with shoelace

1 Number the pages of your book at the top, alternating paper colors. Number your first page very lightly, so you can erase it when you bind.

2 With your bone folder, trace your cup curve at the same place on the back of each page.

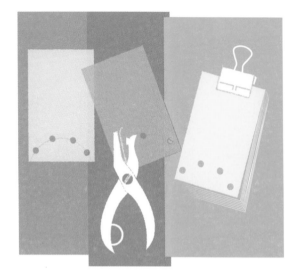

3 Punch 3–4 holes on each curve, alternating hole placement so that they do not show through from page to page.

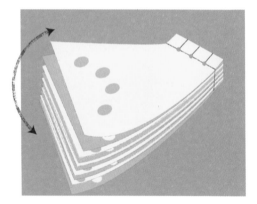

NOTE: For flip books, images need to be at the bottom third of the paper, so that they show when you flip the book.

4 Pile the pieces up, fanning the bottom just a bit for ease when flipping. Clip or rubber-band to test your flip book. Rearrange your pages if necessary so that the balls move when you flip your book.

5 When you are happy with your flip book, clip it to stabilize your pages while you punch and sew.

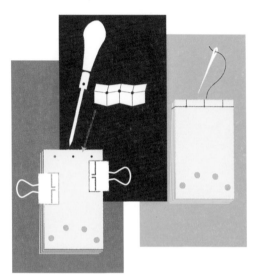

6 Make a template for punching your holes (see below). Use your awl to make three holes through the whole book about ½" (1.3 cm) from the top. Stab-stitch (see page 132).

Stitching Hole Template

1 Cut a piece of scrap paper the width of your spine by about 2" (5 cm) long.

2 Fold it about ½" (1.3 cm) from the top.

3 Fold it in half in the other direction (to find the center).

4 Fold one end in about ½" (1.3 cm)—match that with other end.

Punch your stitching holes where those folds intersect.

Bouncing Ball Variation

Punch your holes in other patterns instead of following the traced cup, making sure that the holes alternate from page to page.

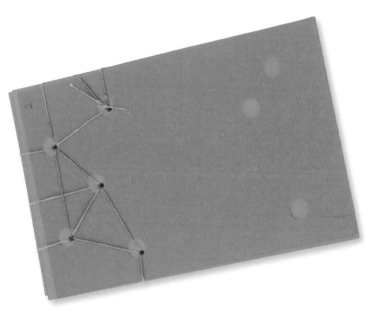

NOTE: For a large quantity of stab-stitch, you can make stitching holes with a hand drill, clamping to a board to stabilize your pages before you drill. The first time we drilled paper with an electric drill it spun around wild—very unsettling—but also sort of interesting.

Stitch Variation

Once you understand stab-stitching, you can invent your own stitching pattern—or even stitch with a random pattern, improvising as you go!

Variation for Younger Children

Make a two-hole template and punch each page. Tie with a shoelace. You can tie with a square knot—left over right and right over left—or use a bow so that you can untie and change the order of your pages for fun.

Stab-Stitching

1 Thread the needle, locking the thread through the tail (see page 109).

2 Start at the middle hole on the back of your book, leaving about a 3" (7.6 cm) tail of thread to tie later. **A**

3 Stitch around the spine and come back through the same hole. **B, C**

4 Stitch through the next hole, stitch around the spine, and come back through the same hole. **D, E, F**

5 Stitch around the side and come back through the same hole. **G, H**

6 Stitch through the middle hole and head up to your last hole. **I**

7 Stitch through the last hole, bring your needle around the spine, and then bring it back through the same hole. **J, K, L**

8 Stitch around the side and come back through the same hole. **M, N, O**

9 Pluck your thread to check tension. If it's loose, adjust by tugging the thread through the holes like tightening your shoelaces. **P**

10 Tie your thread to the tail with a square knot—left over right, right over left—centering your knot on the back middle hole. **Q**

11 Check tension again. If necessary, untie and adjust your tension before you trim the thread.

12 Trim the thread to 1" (2.5 cm) or so. Comb out the thread with the needle if you like. Trim a little closer.

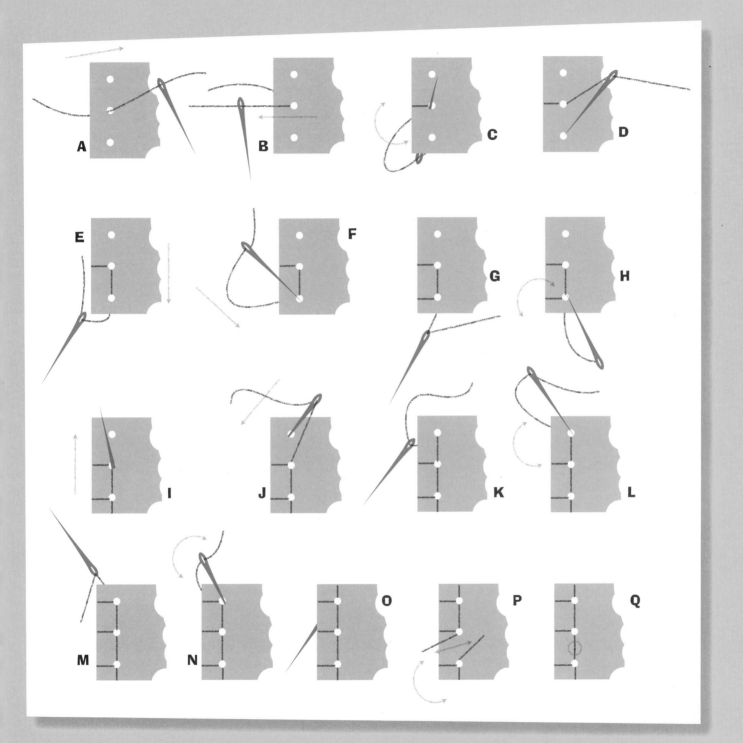

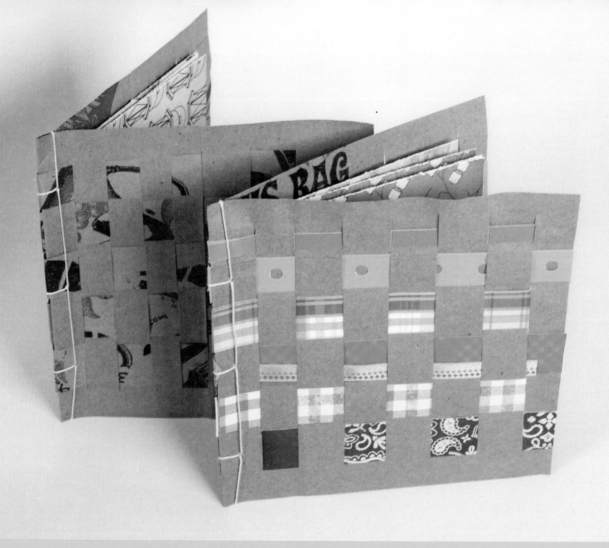

Woven Paper Bag Book

It can be hard to find paper big enough to cover your book. I remember that this happened when I wrote a children's book for my kiddie lit class when I was in college. I had typed it onto regular business-size paper, but needed something more than twice as big for the cover—so I wove together a few paper bags.

materials

paper bags, or heavy wrapping paper,
    butcher paper, etc., more than twice as
    large as your pages—use the same color
    bags for a subtle woven texture or bags in
    contrasting colors if you would like to see
    the checkered pattern of the weaving
book pages
scissors
adhesives (glue stick, double-stick tape, etc.)
awl
needle and thread

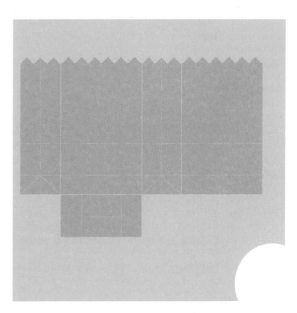

1 With great care, unmake your paper bags—trimming near the glue points as needed, trimming out the bottom, etc. There are various kinds of bags, so pay attention to how yours was put together. This also shows you how to make a bag, in case you ever need to do that!

2 Lay your unmade bag on a table. Put your pages on top, and wrap the bag around them to see how big it needs to be.

5 Leaving a little space on the top, bottom, and edges, cut strips into your paper, starting at the fold. These strips do not get cut all the way across; in a sense, you are making both the loom and warp of your paper weaving.

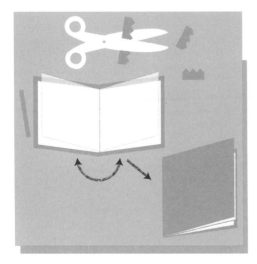

3 Trim the bag to the size you will need for your cover. Try it out and trim carefully to fit—just a bit larger than your book on all sides. Leave plenty of room for your book's spine.

4 Fold this piece in half as shown. Remove your book pages.

6 With your other (contrasting color if you chose those) bags, cut strips the height of your cover. These can be the same or different widths, and they can be in as many colors as you like.

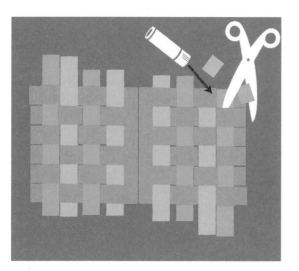

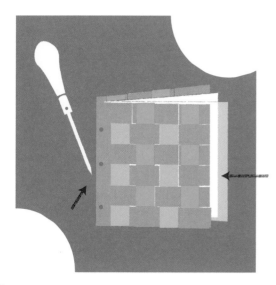

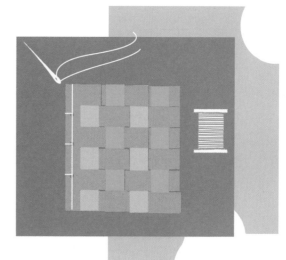

7 Weave the strips in and out of your big piece, alternating over and under. Alternate the colors if you are using several.

8 Glue down the ends so that your weaving does not slip out. Trim the ends flush with the cover.

9 Fold your woven cover around your pages. Punch three holes with an awl, as shown.

10 Stab-stitch (see page 132).

Resources

Your best resources are your local bookstores, art-supply stores, printers, and libraries.

Use them (so you don't lose them!)

Art Supplies

FineArtStore.com
Fine papers and bookbinding supplies

Jo-Ann Fabric and Craft Stores
Craft and art supplies, multiple store locations
www.joann.com

New York Central Art Supply
Excellent paper department
www.nycentralart.com

Paper Source
Custom printing, extensive paper collection, book-making supplies
Author has signed books at many locations
www.papersource.com

Royalwood, Ltd. Online
Waxed linen thread in many colors
www.royalwoodltd.com

Talas
Bookbinding tools and supplies
www.talasonline.com

Recommended Books

600 Black Spots: Pop-up Book for Children of All Ages
David A. Carter
Little Simon, New York, NY
© 2007

The Absolutely True Diary of a Part-Time Indian
Sherman Alexi and Ellen Forney
Little, Brown and Company
New York, NY
© 2007

Beautiful Oops!
Barney Saltzberg
Workman Publishing, New York, NY
© 2010

Find the Constellations
H. A. Rey
Houghton Mifflin, New York, NY
© 1956

Happy Birthday: A Very Special Little Golden Book with Party Cut-Outs, Favors, Games, Invitations, Place Cards, Candy Cups
Simon & Schuster; 1st THUS edition (1952)
New York, NY
Rare 1952 edition

Harold & the Purple Crayon
Crocket Johnson
HarperCollins Publishers
New York, NY
© 1955

Just us Women
Jeannette Caines and Pat Cummings
HarperCollins Children's Books
New York, NY
© 1982

Little Bear's Friend
Else Holmelund Minarik, Maurice Sendak
Harper & Row
© 1960

The Little Fur Family
Margaret Wise Brown, Garth Williams
Harper Bros (1946–2003)
New York, NY
© 1946

The Nutshell Library
Maurice Sendak
Harper & Row (1962–1990)
© 1962

Oscar-the-Grouch's Alphabet of Trash
Jeffrey Moss and Sal Murdocca
Western Publishing Company, Inc.
© 1978

*Playing with Color: 50 Graphic Experiments
for Exploring Color Design*
Richard Mehl
Rockport Publishers, Beverly, MA
© 2013

*Playing with Sketches: 50 Creative Exercises
for Designers and Artists*
Whitney Sherman
Rockport Publishers, Beverly, MA
© 2013

*Pop-Up: Everything You Need to Create Your
Own Pop-Up Book*
Ruth Wickings and Frances Castle
Candlewick Press, Somerville, MA
© 2010

See the Circus
H. A. Rey
Houghton Mifflin, New York, NY
© 1956

The Rainy Day Play Book
Marion Conger and Natalie Young
Golden Press
© 1951

Esther K Smith Books

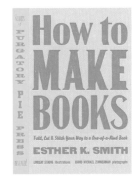

*How to Make Books:
Fold, Cut & Stitch Your Way to a
One-of-a-Kind Book*
Esther K Smith
Potter Craft, New York, NY
November 2007

*Magic Books & Paper Toys: Flip Books, E-Z Pop-Ups
& Other Paper Playthings to Amaze & Delight*
Esther K Smith
Potter Craft, New York, NY
November 2008

Author Classes

LIKE Purgatory Pie Press on Facebook for
information on author events
www.Purgatorypiepress.com
www.estherksmith.com

Bring Esther K Smith to your local center to
teach a class.

Past & Future Workshops

McNally Jackson Books
www.mcnallyjackson.com

Greenlight Book Store
www.greenlightbookstore.com

Word
www.wordbookstores.com

Brooklyn Book Festival
www.brooklynbookfestival.org

....
(Your favorite bookstore's name here!)

Acknowledgments

First, thanks to Whitney Sherman, who introduced me to Emily Potts, who liked this idea best and sent me to the amazing Joy Aquilino, Betsy Gammons, Anne Re, and Lara Neel—thanks for all of your hard work. And thanks to the Quarto sales team and to all the people behind the scenes who made this book.

谨谢于中国协助我印刷与装帧此书的人们

Thanks again Marianne Merola, Alicia Bay Laurel, Scott McCarney, Beth Sheehan, Abby Schoolman, Anne Marion-Gallois, Urszula Glogowska, Kyle A. Holland, Jennifer King, Nikki Lee, Malgosia Kostecka, Debra Eck, April Vollmer, Liz Grace, Ha Young Kim, Gertjan van Kempen, Naftali Rottenstreich, Dayna Burnett, Allan Bealy, and as always to my family—
AND to everyone I forgot.

Thanks for having me make books with kids:

MAD Museum of Arts & Design
Cooper Hewitt National Design Museum
Liz Koch at the Brooklyn Book Festival
Yvonne Brooks and McNally Jackson Books
Jessica Stockton Bagnulo and Rebecca Fitting
    at the Greenlight Bookstore
Christine Onorati at Word Bookstores
Kristie Valentine at Cathedral School
Joan Kim when you were at 826NYC
Stephanie Trejo, Ann Coffin, and Kirsten
    Flaherty at IPCNY (I found pop-ups,
    page 86, left on floor after workshop)

Jane Sanders: It was so much fun to get to work with you and your illustrations—and thanks to your family, Elizabeth and Howard.

Thanks, Pat Lee, for your preliminary copy editing and proofreading—and for your appreciation of cephalopods—and for your discretion.

Editor, Christina Penambuco-Holsten, thanks again for helping me with our fourth book together—and again and again for the other three.

Many people helped photograph this book. Thanks to Wyatt Counts, Emma Andreetti, Michael Bartalos, Michael Prisco, and Han Ju Chou.

Thanks so much to my design collaborators: Amy Sly, Jane Treuhaft, and Robin Sherin.

Thanks to University of Chicago for our intelligent, capable, humorous, creative interns and externs. And thanks again Mateo Pomi, Megan Anderluh, Jen Xue for all your help with this book.

Book Artists

Jane Sanders made most of the book projects.
I made a few (pages 37, 54, 57, 128, 131).

Thanks for making books for this book:

Michael Bartalos & Bruno Bartalos, pages 42, 46
www.bartalosillustration.com

Mindell Dubansky, page 117
aboutblooks.blogspot.com

Colette Fu, pages 68, 83
www.colettefu.com

Susan Happersett
pages 6, 50, 64, cover
fibonaccisusan.com

Miriam Schaer, page 122
www.miriamschaer.com

Cassie Elton, page 121
Liam and Aiden Kelley, page 26
Caroline Reilly, page 86 top
Jen Xue, pages 35, 60, 62, 127, cover

And thanks Georgia Luna (pages 7, 34, 87, cover) and Polly EllaNora for being my kids and making books with me forever and for bringing your friends, Shanelle Hudson, Willy Naess, Molly Rosner (page 30), and Lila Yip.

And thanks for your project ideas:

Elise Engler, page 118
www.eliseengler.com

Jean Kropper, page 60
www.paperandpixel.com.au

Jennifer Verbit, page 54

And thanks to the children who came over to make books with me at my big yellow table: Lila Stevens, pages 37, 87, Basia Panko, page 87, and Heloise Rifflet who called me Estelle Pastel.

141

Index

Esther K Smith, author of *How to Make Books*, has made books with kids at Cooper Hewitt Museum, MAD Museum of Arts & Design, 826 NYC, many bookstores, and every year at the Brooklyn Book Festival. The book Esther is hugging is H. A. Rey's flap book, *See the Circus*.

Dikko Faust, Type-O-Graphics

Dikko handsets large, wooden type and small, metal type and prints it at Purgatory Pie Press in New York City. Dikko teaches letterpress printmaking at the School of Visual Arts. He handset and printed the wood display type for *Making Books with Kids* and Esther K Smith's three other books.

Esther K Smith and Dikko Faust make books at Purgatory Pie Press in New York City, (www. purgatorypiepress.com), collaborating with other artists and writers. Their limited editions and artist books are in the permanent collections at the Metropolitan Museum of Art, MoMA: Museum of Modern Art, The Cooper Hewitt National Design Museum, the Victoria & Albert Museum, and many other museums and rare book libraries throughout the world.

Jane Sanders, illustrator, grew up in Chapel Hill, North Carolina. She studied at the North Carolina School of the Arts and Parsons School of Design. Her illustrations have appeared in the *New York Times*, *Highlights* magazine, MoMA: Museum of Modern Art greeting cards, and toy packages. Jane recently won a They Draw & Travel award for a map of her neighborhood in Queens. She also animates her drawings. One of her animations was on a Jumbotron in New York's Times Square. See more of her work at www.reddozer.com.

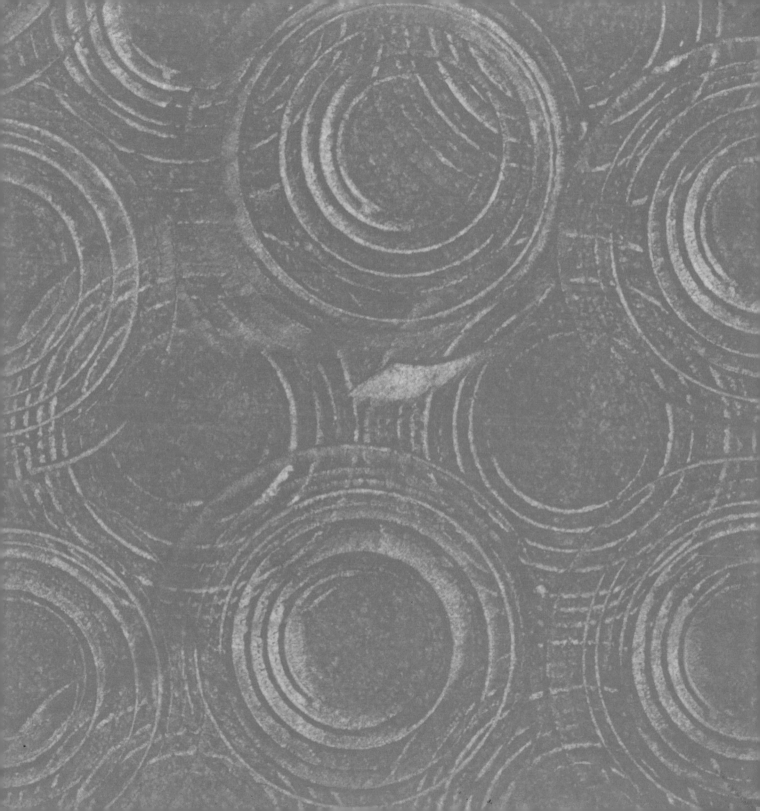